ULTIMATE SUPERSTARS

HARRY STYLES

AN UNOFFICIAL STORY

First published in the UK in 2025 by Studio Press,
an imprint of Bonnier Books UK,
5th Floor, HYLO, 105 Bunhill Row, London, EC1Y 8LZ

www.bonnierbooks.co.uk

Text © Studio Press 2025
Written by Dan Whitehead
Cover illustration by Julia Murray

All rights reserved. No part of this publication may be reproduced, stored in a retrieval system, or transmitted in any form or by any means, without the prior permission in writing of the publisher, nor be otherwise circulated in any form of binding or cover other than that in which it is published and without a similar condition including this condition being imposed on the subsequent purchaser.

Paperback ISBN: 978-1-83587-300-7

British Library cataloguing-in-publication data: A catalogue record for this book is available from the British Library.

Printed and bound in Great Britain by Clays Ltd, Elcograf S.p.A.

1 3 5 7 9 10 8 6 4 2

The authorised representative in the EEA is Bonnier Books UK (Ireland) Limited.

Registered office address: Floor 3, Block 3, Miesian Plaza
50–58 Baggot Street Lower, Dublin 2, D02 Y754, Ireland.
compliance@bonnierbooks.ie

The views in this book are the author's own and the copyright, trademarks and names are that of their respective owners and are not intended to suggest endorsement, agreement, affiliation or otherwise of any kind.

This book is unofficial and unauthorised and is not endorsed by or affiliated with Harry Styles.

ULTIMATE SUPERSTARS

HARRY STYLES

AN UNOFFICIAL STORY

CONTENTS

CHAPTER 1 – A HEADLINE ACT 9

CHAPTER 2 – A CHRISTMAS GIFT 16

CHAPTER 3 – WHITE ESKIMO 22

CHAPTER 4 – SHOOTING FOR THE STARS 29

CHAPTER 5 – A STROKE OF LUCK 38

CHAPTER 6 – FROM BOYS TO BOY BAND 46

CHAPTER 7 – JUST THE BEGINNING 52

CHAPTER 8 – *X FACTOR* ON THE ROAD........59

CHAPTER 9 – ONE DIRECTION GOES GLOBAL 65

CHAPTER 10 – ONE DIRECTION FEVER 70

CHAPTER 11	– BRUSHING SHOULDERS WITH THE STARS	78
CHAPTER 12	– MAKE HAY WHILE THE SUN SHINES	86
CHAPTER 13	– AROUND THE WORLD	93
CHAPTER 14	– AND THEN THERE WERE FOUR	101
CHAPTER 15	– ONE LAST SONG	108
CHAPTER 16	– MEET HARRY	114
CHAPTER 17	– MUSIC I WANT TO MAKE	120
CHAPTER 18	– READY, SET, RELEASE	127
CHAPTER 19	– MADISON SQUARE GARDEN	134
CHAPTER 20	– FEATHER BOAS FOR EVERYONE	143

CHAPTER 1

A HEADLINE ACT

The sound of church bells rang out across the Coachella Valley in California. It was late in the evening of 15 April 2022 and the first day of the Coachella music festival was well underway. In the dark of the stage, Harry Styles waited patiently. The enormous crowd was still buzzing from the performance by Canadian singer Daniel Caesar, who had brought on none other than Justin Bieber as a surprise guest. The headline act for this opening night would really have to deliver something amazing to top that.

As Harry's rabbit-themed intro video ended and the lights came up, the 28-year-old star stood, proud and silent, as the crowd roared in excitement. He was wearing a huge fluffy black coat, which he then threw off to reveal a sequinned sleeveless jumpsuit underneath. His musical heroes as a kid had been Elvis Presley, Elton John and Freddie Mercury – big personalities who dressed the part and put on a spectacular show. That was what he intended to do.

Unable to keep his serious face any longer, Harry beamed a joyful smile and bounded down the steps, launching straight into 'As It Was', his latest single. It was like someone had run electricity through the festival field and everyone started bouncing up and down in time to the music.

The song gave Harry something to focus on, and he needed it. He was no stranger to playing in front of big crowds, but this was on a whole new level. His thoughts flashed back to the very first time he'd ever appeared on TV, interviewed in Manchester before his first *X Factor* audition. He'd described his hometown of Holmes Chapel in Cheshire as 'boring but picturesque', and he couldn't help thinking of it now. The entire population of the town where he'd grown up was barely 5,000. Now he was headlining one of America's biggest rock festivals in front of over 100,000 people.

Playing Coachella was a big deal, and even more so in 2022. The whole world was just coming out of lockdown as a result of the Covid-19 pandemic. This was the first time the festival had taken place since 2019. Just being at this show would have been a massive validation of Harry's rock-star credentials. But being chosen as the opening night headliner? The idea made his head spin.

Previous headliners had included Prince, Lady Gaga, Beyonce, Radiohead and Eminem. Even Paul McCartney of The Beatles! Less than ten years ago, Harry had been a pop-obsessed teenager, finishing his GCSEs and dreaming of singing for a living. Now? He was walking the same stage as the legends who had inspired him. He'd truly made it.

It was a moment that threatened to overwhelm him, but Harry kept the energy high, rolling straight into 'Adore You', then 'Golden' followed by 'Carolina'. He knew these songs back to front, but so did the thousands of people in front of the stage, all singing along with him. Their love gave Harry even more confidence, driving him to push even harder with his performance.

He'd barely even spoken to the crowd, he'd been so thrilled to just keep singing. "This is a new song," he said, as he prepared to sing 'Boyfriends'. The crowd went nuts! "You 'aven't even heard it yet!" he laughed. Most pop stars are worried about debuting new material to crowds who love the hits, but the overwhelming positive response reassured Harry that the Coachella audience was ready to come along with him wherever he wanted to lead them. And that was good, as he had a few surprises lined up.

He effortlessly held the crowd in the palm of his hand. He drew them in close for the acoustic ballad, 'Cherry', and brought his backing band up alongside him. He promised them exactly twelve minutes of dancing as he delivered a medley of 'She' and 'Canyon Moon', jigging excitedly around the stage, spinning around, lost in the experience. Now came the moment he knew the crowd would go bananas for. He'd built them up to it, and as soon as the first bars of One Direction's 'What Makes You Beautiful' hit, it was like the whole festival exploded. Harry's soaring voice joined with the thousands of fans singing along. He'd always worried about moving on from being a member of a huge boy band to being a solo artist. Would people still like him? Belting out the biggest 1D hit made those worries melt away. The lights blazed. The music lifted him. He was owning his past.

It was a glorious, triumphant moment, and for most stars that would have been the perfect point to end the show, with the audience still buzzing from a blast of pop perfection. But Harry didn't like to do the obvious. The stage was quiet, people were beginning to wonder if that was the last song, when the horn players in his band suddenly pierced the silence with a familiar musical sting. Harry, ever the showman, pretended to be confused. What was happening? They played the sting again. It was the intro to 'Man, I Feel Like A Woman', the chart-topping 1997 hit by Shania Twain.

And now there she was, rising from the stairs at the back of the stage, wearing a sequinned dress that matched Harry's jumpsuit. This was the part of the show that Harry was *really* excited about. He'd been a little kid when this song was originally a hit, and one of his first musical memories was singing along to it in the car with his mum. Now he was covering it, alongside Shania Twain herself, a dream come true!

And still Harry wasn't finished! He played another new song, 'Late Night Talking', and 'Watermelon Sugar', which always got the crowd hyped – not that they needed it. He rocked out for an extended version of 'Kiwi', and finally ended the night with a majestic version of 'Sign Of The Times'. Fireworks blazed as the song reached its emotional peak, matching the jubilant thrill Harry felt. He looked out at the sea of eager faces and thanked them. This wasn't just the obligatory farewell that pop stars give at the end of a show, but a heartfelt connection. This had been a truly special experience for Harry, a triumphant, flawless performance that showed the world – and even himself – that he belonged on the biggest stage.

The Coachella festival runs for a whole week, with the headliners all returning for another show the following weekend. The knowledge that he'd get to do this all over again thrilled Harry. But even more than that; as he walked off stage, exhausted but elated, knowing he would get to deliver performances like this for the rest of his life made him feel complete and content.

CHAPTER 2

A CHRISTMAS GIFT

Anne Twist looked down at the gurgling little baby in her arms. It was 1 February 1994. A Tuesday. How did the old rhyme go? Monday's child is fair of face, Tuesday's child is full of grace. As she gazed adoringly at her newborn son, she wondered if he'd been born a day late. With a mop of curly hair and wide eager eyes, he was definitely fair of face. Who knows, maybe he'll be graceful as well! she thought.

With a daughter called Gemma already in the family, she and her partner, Des Styles, had been secretly hoping for a boy. And here he was. Des went from the Alexandra Hospital in Redditch, Worcestershire, to the registrar's office to officially record the birth: Harry Edward Styles had arrived.

Shortly after Harry's birth, the family moved 80 miles north to the small Cheshire town of Holmes Chapel. Quiet and peaceful, and surrounded by farmland, it was the perfect place for the kids to grow up. Several happy years passed until finally Harry was old enough to start nursery.

The staff at Happy Days were immediately smitten with the cheeky, energetic young lad. Some of them would even babysit him in the evenings, as Anne worked running a pub. Harry made friends easily, charming other children and adults alike.

Anne marvelled at how chilled out he was for a toddler. Every morning, as she dropped Harry off, she was struck by how confidently he took it all in his stride. While other kids his age were teary-eyed at the door and crying for their parents to come back, Harry would give her a kiss and a wave, and cheerfully trundle off to paint, or make things or sing and dance. There was definitely a creative spark in him, she thought. The idea that he'd one day end up on stage popped into her head more than once, and it somehow seemed quite natural.

The years went by, and soon enough Harry

was starting at primary school, looking smart and adorable in his uniform. Even there he continued to be friendly and popular. Unlike other boys his age, he was also happy to make friends with girls – and even had a few girlfriends despite his young age!

While Harry was having fun, things weren't going quite so well at home. Anne and Des had realised their relationship wasn't working. One day, they sat seven-year-old Harry and his older sister Gemma down on the sofa in the living room and broke the news: "We're splitting up." This was something that even Harry's upbeat personality struggled to take in, and he burst into tears immediately.

It wasn't quite the massive change Harry expected, at least not immediately. Des still lived with them, sleeping in the spare room, for two years before finally moving out. Even then, he would spend weekends with his kids. He'd put on his favourite records, big catchy rock songs by Elvis and Queen, and Harry would sing along. Music was more than just something fun to listen to. These songs were part of a family ritual that made him feel happy.

Harry loved belting out these retro hits so much

that he started to seek out opportunities to sing whenever and wherever he could. One Christmas, he eyed the large, wrapped box with his name on it eagerly. It was a present from his grandad, and he hoped with all his heart that it was what he thought it was. He loved football, he loved riding his bike, but there was one thing he wanted above everything else.

When Christmas morning finally came, he tore off the colourful paper in a frenzy. "Yes!" he shouted as what was inside revealed itself. His very own karaoke machine! Now he could sing along to whatever he wanted, and with the built-in microphone everyone could hear him! The family was treated to a private concert that very day, unaware that in less than ten years' time millions of people would dream of such a treat.

Harry wanted to do more than just perform for his family. Whenever school plays came up, he'd volunteer enthusiastically, loving the chance to be on stage even if it was just the small makeshift one in the school hall, with cardboard sets and homemade costumes. The chance to dress up, pretending to be someone else, making people laugh, it gave him a feeling like nothing he'd ever experienced.

Entertaining people came easily to him. He seemed to know exactly how to say a line to make people laugh, or how to win the crowd over with a smile or a wink. Though he was too young to put it into words, he felt like he'd found the thing he was meant to do, a talent that made him as happy as the audience. It was an amazing feeling.

When the school put on their version of *Chitty Chitty Bang Bang*, Harry got to play Buzz Lightyear, a toy who had come to life and was hiding from the sinister Child Catcher. He dressed up as a mouse for another play. He didn't care about looking silly, he didn't mind that the parts he played may not always have been 'cool'. It was all about that thrill of stepping out into the lights and letting the creativity flow through him. Every time he took a bow at the end of a new show, to rapturous applause from friends and their families, something inside of him lit up. *I want to do this again... and again and again!* he thought.

But the school only put on a few plays every year, and even for someone as popular and talented as Harry, there was no guarantee he'd get a part in each one. His hunger for performance would need something more to satisfy it. He needed an excuse to put on a show whenever he wanted, without relying on teachers to make it happen. As luck would have it, as Harry moved from primary to secondary school, he was about to embark on a friendship that would deliver exactly this...

CHAPTER 3

WHITE ESKIMO

"Hiya, I'm Will!" Harry hadn't been at Holmes Chapel Comprehensive for long before a tall, excitable boy in his year introduced himself. The friendly face of Will Sweeny came as a welcome relief.

"I'm Harry," he replied, shaking Will's outstretched hand. It was a small and simple moment, but one that would change the course of Harry's life – he just didn't know it yet!

The change from primary to secondary school had been harder than he expected. In his final year at primary school, he'd been one of the most popular kids in a school with only a few hundred pupils. Now he was just another nervous 11-year-old in a school with over a thousand pupils. Some of the older lads even had moustaches!

Harry and Will quickly became best mates and would spend almost all of their free time hanging out at each other's houses. They laughed at the same jokes, liked the same music, even fancied the same girls most of the time. They clicked together immediately, like jigsaw pieces.

Also, like Harry, Will's parents had split up when he was younger. Harry was fascinated by the fact that Will's mum, Yvette, was a celebrity. She'd been a Blue Peter presenter when she was just 18 and now travelled around the country making popular ghost-hunting shows for TV. She'd been born and had grown up around the same small Cheshire towns as Harry. If she could get on the telly, Harry often wondered to himself, then what's stopping me from doing the same?

Harry wasn't interested in presenting TV shows though. He'd got his heart set on music, and it just so happened that Will had similar ambitions. "We should start a band," Will declared one day. Will would be the drummer, with their other friends Haydn Morris and Nick Clough on bass and guitar.

That just left one job in the band open for Harry.

"I'm not sure I want to be the singer," Harry insisted.

Will rolled his eyes. "Mate, you've got a great voice. You're always singing anyway. What's the difference?"

Now that it was something could really happen, Harry felt self-conscious. The idea of going from singing along to his karaoke machine at home to singing in front of an audience suddenly felt like a big step. This wasn't the primary school nativity anymore!

"OK, I'll do it," said Harry. A flutter of nerves and excitement tickled his insides. He was committed to it now. They just needed a name. Will, Haydn and Nick all bounced around different ideas. "What about White Eskimo?" asked Harry. He'd always been good at putting random words together in a way that sounded cool. None of them knew what it meant, but it sounded good. It sounded like the name of a band.

White Eskimo practised in the school's cramped music room after school.

"Hey, we're pretty good," said Will. Harry cringed. They'd been taping their rehearsals and listening to themselves after each session. It was the first time Harry had heard his singing played back to him. It sounded weird. "You sound great!" said Will, reassuringly. "Everyone thinks their voice is horrible when they hear it recorded."

All of them were a little surprised how quickly they learned to work together, keeping in time and in tune, slowly learning the chords for songs they could play. They were particularly good at performing 'Summer of '69', a hit from 1985 by the Canadian rock star Bryan Adams. The passionate tone suited Harry's vocal style, and it quickly became one of their favourites. They'd practise other cover versions as well, such as the 1960s pop song 'Valleri', originally a hit for The Monkees.

Harry was intrigued by the story of The Monkees. The band had been put together by Hollywood TV producers, who auditioned actors and musicians to create an American pop band that could compete with The Beatles. They even had their own TV show. They reminded Harry of modern boy bands, created in much the same way by people like Simon Cowell and Louis Walsh on *The X Factor*. Harry loved that show. He'd watch it every week, arguing with his family over who was best, and secretly imagining he was the one auditioning. He even looked up how to apply, but you had to be at least 16 and Harry wasn't quite there yet.

White Eskimo started out by playing gigs at school to audiences made up of their classmates. They'd lug all their instruments and equipment into the school hall or cafeteria, take off their blazers and loosen their ties. Harry had taken to wearing a red headband on stage. "It makes me look like a proper rock star!" he insisted when his bandmates teased him about it.

It didn't take long for them to be asked to perform outside of school. They took their fairly well-polished set and performed it at a wedding. Harry ditched the headband for this gig and they all wore suits – it didn't seem very cool to turn up in school uniform! Harry half expected the wedding guests to complain, maybe even boo them offshouting: "This isn't a real band! These are just teenagers!" But instead everyone clapped and danced and treated them like professional musicians.

When their school announced it would be holding a Battle of the Bands, all the lads knew they had to enter. While they still mostly covered other people's songs, they'd been writing and rehearsing their own material. White Eskimo was also developing its own unique sound, a sort of poppy punky upbeat indie rock that always seemed to get people jumping up and down.

On the day of the Battle of the Bands, they debated what to play. In the end, they decided to stick with the song they knew they could absolutely smash – 'Summer of '69'. They belted it out, Harry grabbing the mic like a true star. But the other bands were good as well. The votes were counted. The announcement came. White Eskimo was officially the best band at Holmes Chapel Comprehensive!

That night, still buzzing from the victory, Harry wrestled with a huge decision. He'd turned 16 now. He'd soon be finished with school forever. He could finally apply for *The X Factor*. Winning the Battle of the Bands had convinced him that he stood a pretty good chance of at least getting to the auditions. It was something he'd dreamed of for years. But every time he went to submit his application, he chickened out at the last minute. What if they just rejected him straight away? What if he got through but the judges hated him? Worse, what if the audience hated him?

Harry's mum, Anne, knew what he was going through. They'd talked about it so many times. Sitting together, watching *The X Factor*, she'd seen singers with less talent and charisma than her son get through. He just needed a little push to believe in himself. After hearing he'd backed out of applying one time too many, she made her move. She submitted the application for him. She'd known he was a star from the day he was born. It was time the rest of the world knew it as well.

CHAPTER 4

SHOOTING FOR THE STARS

Harry Styles took a deep breath. In just a few moments his life would change forever — he just wasn't sure how. Standing backstage at the Manchester Central Arena, the 16-year-old was surrounded by his family, all wearing custom-made T-shirts. *We think Harry has the X Factor* they read. All he had to do was take a few steps forward, out onto the stage in front of thousands of people, and he'd find out if that was true.

He gripped his microphone tightly. Dermot O'Leary, the presenter, was saying something, but he couldn't hear him. He was thinking how only a few years ago the biggest performance he'd ever given was in his school canteen. Now he was going to sing, live on television as a contestant on *The X Factor*, watched by millions of people. His stomach flipped with a mixture of nerves and excitement. Suddenly there was a flurry of activity, Dermot was ushering him towards the stage, his family grabbing and hugging him for one last good-luck wish.

The stage felt enormous, but Harry walked out casually, as if this was something he did every day. He'd worn a grey cardigan over a plain white T-shirt, with black cargo trousers and boots. A stylishly thin scarf looped loosely around his neck. That was his style. Comfy but cool.

Peering against the bright lights, he could just make out the rows and rows of seats, all filled with *X Factor* fans who had come to see who would be judged worthy of appearing on the show. And in front of the crowd, sitting at their famous table, were Louis Walsh, Nicole Scherzinger and Simon Cowell. It was a sight he'd seen dozens of times on the TV. Now they were really there – and looking at him!

Harry introduced himself, and his heart leapt at the cheers from the crowd when he said his name. He heard himself explaining how he works Saturdays at the local bakery in Holmes Chapel, the town where he lived. It was like he was outside himself, in a dream.

Simon asked a question, but Harry couldn't hear him. "Eh?" He leaned forward, like he was talking to a customer in the shop, not one of the most powerful men in pop.

"What's popular in the bakery?" Simon wanted to know.

"Viennese Fancies!" Harry quipped, quick as a flash. "Always a favourite." The crowd laughed, already loving his easy-going personality and cheeky charm.

Then Simon asked what wasn't popular in the bakery world. Harry gave an exaggerated pause, hands on hips as he pondered this question as if it was the most serious thing in the universe. "White Coburg," he finally declared, giving a theatrical thumbs-down. Even Simon Cowell laughed at this. "It's a white loaf, like a circle," Harry continued. "It's got a cross on the top," he added with a twinkle in his eye, as if explaining baked goods to a small child. This got an even bigger laugh.

Harry was in the zone now. He explained how he'd always been a fan of *The X Factor* but hadn't been old enough to apply until now. Secretly, he thought about how he'd filled out his application but had chickened out of sending it. It was his mum, Anne, who had finally sent it in, knowing that her talented son would shine when given the chance. He didn't tell the judges about his cold feet, but he did tell them that he wanted to find out if he had what it takes to be a real pop star, adding that his mum thought he was a good singer.

Simon rolled his eyes at this, looking knowingly at the audience. He'd heard that line thousands of times. "Mums usually *don't* know," he said, witheringly.

But Harry wasn't put off. "Yeah, that's what I mean!" He gestured excitedly to the judges. "That's why I wanted to come and ask from the people who know."

It was the honest truth. He loved singing. He felt like he was pretty good at it. But was he 'pop star' good? It was time to prove that there was more to Harry Styles than a winning personality. He'd chosen 'Hey Soul Sister' by Train as his performance piece.

Did Simon look bored at the song choice? Harry couldn't tell, but at least Louis Walsh was excited. "That's my favourite song in the charts," he said, beaming.

The music started up, and Harry began to sing. He knew the song inside out. He'd practiced it over and over. He was giving it his all, hitting the notes. This was the bit he loved. Singing was great. Singing in front of people was even better. But he was also very aware that this was no ordinary singalong. He wasn't crooning in the shower or for his schoolmates now. This was make or break.

Past the first verse and into the chorus. He knew what he was singing was good... but not great. He prowled the stage, not even looking at the audience. The confident lad of a few minutes ago seemed to have disappeared. It was a song but not really a performance. The show was well titled... and whatever 'X Factor' they were looking for, Harry could sense it wasn't happening. Frustration began to rise, clouding his thoughts.

The music stopped. Simon Cowell had halted the performance halfway through. Harry's heart sank.

Was that it? Had he blown it already?

"I think the track might be throwing you off," said Simon. "Can I hear something that's just you, with no music?"

Singing in front of thousands of people is one thing. Singing acapella, just his voice with no music to guide him? That was a scary prospect at the best of times. The pressure was really on now. But from somewhere deep inside, Harry felt his confidence surge. He told the judges that instead he'd sing 'Isn't She Lovely', a 1976 soul ballad by Stevie Wonder, one of the greatest singers in history. It was a bold choice but it wasn't cockiness that made him pick it. He just knew in his gut that this was the one. This would let him sing from the heart.

There's a moment of silence, and Harry begins to sing again. This time there's no music. Although there are thousands of people in the huge arena, it's perfectly quiet except for Harry's voice filling the space. This time he's truly lost in the music. It's a song about a middle-aged father seeing his baby daughter for the first time, but somehow a 16-year-old boy who had only just finished his GCSEs made it sound like this wave of incredible emotion was happening to him, right now.

Harry finished to applause and cheers. He still didn't know if he had that mysterious 'X Factor', but he knew he couldn't have given any more than he just did. This was the performance he needed to give, and he'd given it. He waited nervously on the stage, suddenly feeling very vulnerable and exposed, as the judges gave their feedback.

"You have a beautiful voice," said Nicole Scherzinger, sending Harry's mood soaring.

Louis agreed that he had a great voice. "However..." Louis continued, "You're so young. I don't think you have the experience or confidence yet."

Harry mumbled "OK" into the microphone. He'd always known this was a long shot, and he tried not to panic, but maybe Louis was right. Maybe it wasn't quite time yet. Maybe he could apply again in a few years...

Someone in the audience shouted "rubbish!" at Louis. There was a ripple of appreciation from the crowd and Harry couldn't help but feel hopeful.

Simon Cowell nodded. "I totally agree with them,"

he said to huge cheers from audience. "With a bit of vocal coaching," Simon continued, "you actually could be very good."

Harry breathed a huge sigh of relief, a bright smile on his face. To get praise like that from one of the fussiest people in the music industry was enormous. Whatever happened next he knew that he was on the right path. He could make it as a pop star.

The judges gave their final verdicts. Louis voted no. The crowd booed. Simon egged the crowd on to boo Louis even louder. His cheeky confidence returning, Harry lifted the microphone to his lips and added a little "boo" of his own into the roar.

"I like you Harry," said Nicole. "I'm going to say yes."

One no and one yes. This was the deciding moment. Simon Cowell, who had reduced so many wannabe stars to quivering jelly, held Harry's future in his hands. "You'll be happy to hear..." he said, "I'm agreeing with Nicole. You're through to the next round!"

Those words rang in Harry's ears. It was if they had been stamped into his brain in giant golden glittering letters. He was going to be on *The X Factor*! As he hurried off stage, babbling heartfelt thank yous into his mic, to be surrounded by hugs and kisses from his family, he knew the journey had begun. It would be long. It would be difficult. But Harry Styles was about to find out if dreams really can come true.

CHAPTER 5

A STROKE OF LUCK

It was July 2010. Harry woke up in the strange surroundings of a London hotel, close to Wembley where the *X Factor* bootcamp was taking place. It was a scary feeling. Apart from sleepovers and the occasional school trip, he'd never been far away from home before. Now he was on his own, about to face one of the toughest audition processes in pop history.

His stomach was doing somersaults on the short journey to the arena. All the contestants who had made it through the open auditions – over 1,000 of them – were gathered together on the stage to greet Simon and Louis. They were the only two judges. Cheryl Cole had been seriously ill with malaria and was recuperating in Los Angeles. Danni Minogue was in Australia with her first baby. Harry had watched *The X Factor* loads of times, but it was clear this year was going to be different.

The first day of bootcamp was brutal. With the contestants split into the four categories – Boys, Girls, Groups and Over 25s – everyone had to perform the same song, depending on which category they were in. For the boys, including Harry, that meant Michael Jackson's 'Man in the Mirror'. It was a song pitched slightly higher than Harry normally sang, but he managed to get through it.

Half the contestants weren't so lucky. Having everyone sing the same songs meant Simon and Louis could quickly spot the ones who didn't have what it took. There were tears backstage, and Harry couldn't help feeling sorry for those who hadn't made it. Coming all this way only to be sent home immediately must be a horrible feeling, he thought.

The second day of bootcamp dawned. Between their performances, all the contestants received intense training from vocal coaches and choreographers so that everyone was at their very best. This meant some of the remaining performers were pushed outside their comfort zone.

Simon and Louis set everyone a challenge to learn a dance routine with the show's top dance expert, Brian Friedman. They wouldn't be judged on this, they were reassured, but it was a chance to show off their unique style and stage presence. This worried Harry. He was very conscious that he didn't really move around on stage that much, preferring to stay close to the mic stand and concentrate on singing.

He wasn't the only one who didn't like the idea. When the time came to perform the routine, one of the contestants, Zayn Malik, refused to come on stage.

"I hate dancing," he said. "I feel like an idiot. I'm not doing it."

In the end, Simon Cowell himself had to leave his podium and talk Zayn into taking part. Harry was caught between thinking it was a crazy thing to risk being kicked out over, and also being impressed that Zayn took a stand. In the end, they all did the dance and it was fine – even if some of the lads did feel a bit silly!

Next up was the part Harry was most confident about: the solo spot. Each contestant got to choose a song from a list of 40 and sing it in their own style. Harry played it safe and chose 'Stop Crying Your Heart Out' by Oasis. It was a simple song, he knew it inside out and there were no tricky bits or high notes that might trip him up. As he finished singing, he tried to read Simon and Louis's expressions. Were they impressed or bored? He was suddenly struck with panic. He'd picked the safe, boring option when he should have chosen a song that showed he could push himself.

Making matters worse was the fact that the bootcamp performances didn't have a live audience this year, because the judging panel was down to just Simon and Louis. Harry missed having a crowd to play off, and he felt nervous and dejected as he came off stage in the large, empty and suddenly very quiet arena.

As the final day of bootcamp loomed, Harry's confidence had taken a knock. The first auditions had been fun. With so many people, all turning up to give it a try, it hadn't felt that different to performing in school talent shows, despite the huge audience. Bootcamp was different. Here, his talent didn't make him unusual. He was surrounded by hundreds of great singers, confident performers, skilled dancers. And they all had the exact same dream as him. Did he stand out in this crowd? He really wasn't sure. More than ever, he wished he had his family and friends around him.

Unexpectedly, all the remaining contestants were summoned on stage together. Simon and Louis were waiting for them, along with Pussycat Dolls star Nicole Scherzinger who had flown in to fill the third judge's seat.

"Guys," Simon said, "We've made a couple of changes..."

Nicole had suggested that the Over-25s category be bumped up to Over-28 in order to get a more even spread of talent through the groups. That meant the competition in the Boys category had just got a lot fiercer. The number of acts going through to the next stage from each category had also gone up: there would be eight picks from each category, not six like in previous years. Harry almost drove himself mad trying to figure out if this meant he had more of a chance or less.

The wait for the final judgement was excruciating. There was so much hanging around as the different groups were ushered on stage to be given the verdict from the judges. The Boys category was judged last, and as they all filed onto the stage, Harry took deep breaths.

Simon broke the silence. "The first person through to the judge's houses… is John Wilding." More names followed. Nicolo Festa. Paije Richardson. With each one announced, Harry knew the odds of his being the next name grew smaller. Simon gave the next name: "Aiden Grimshaw."

Harry was standing right next to Aiden. They'd got on well during bootcamp, both coming from the North West of England. Harry patted his friend on the back as he shook with disbelief. He was genuinely happy for him. The list continued. Marlon McKenzie. Karl Brown. The gap between each name felt like it lasted forever. Matt Cardle. Another amazing singer, Harry thought. He deserved to go through for sure. But that meant there was only one space left. Could it be him? Please? Simon seemed to give an extra long pause before the final name: "Tom Richards." Harry felt like he'd been punched in the stomach. Up and down the line of remaining contestants he could feel the disappointment from each person. They'd come so close, but it wasn't to be. *The X Factor* would continue without them.

They all trooped off stage in shock. The cameras were waiting, of course. Harry had seen so many rejected singers sobbing through what was almost certainly their last ever TV interview. Now it was his turn. He took off his woolly hat and wiped his eyes as tears welled up. He couldn't think straight. "I'm really gutted," was all he managed to say.

The activity settled down. Those who were going through were being ushered away by the production crew to explain what would happen next. Everyone else just had to wait to be taken back to the hotel, and then home. It had been a fun dream while it lasted and, Harry thought to himself, at least he'd got some top-level tuition that he could use to be an even better frontman for White Eskimo. Maybe it wouldn't be so bad to go back to normal old

Holmes Chapel...

Just as Harry was plucking up the courage to phone his mum and tell her the bad news, a member of the production crew came over. The judges had asked for nine of the rejected contestants — five boys and four girls — to return to the stage. And Harry was one of them!

CHAPTER 6

FROM BOYS TO BOY BAND

Harry joined the small group and followed the producer back to the stage. Nobody knew what was happening. He recognised the lads who'd been summoned along with him though. There was Zayn Malik, who'd almost blown it on day one by refusing the dance challenge. Niall Horan, a lad who'd come all the way from Dublin. He'd spotted Liam Payne at the start of bootcamp – he'd been on the show in 2008, and even made it to the judge's house stage before being sent home. And here was Louis Tomlinson, who'd bumped into Harry in the loos a few days earlier!

Harry liked them all, but he didn't really know them that well. What did they have in common, other than being about the same age? He worried that there'd been some sort of mistake, some problem with the filming maybe, and they were about to be told that they wouldn't even appear in the TV episodes already shot.

The two groups lined up on stage, nervously. The girls on the left, the boys on the right. Instinctively, the lads had bundled together, arms around each other's shoulders for friendly support. They looked out at Simon, Louis and Nicole, eager for an explanation.

"Thank you so much for coming back," said Nicole. "We've thought long and hard about it, and we feel you're each too talented to let go of..." Harry tried to make sense of what he was hearing. Was he out or not? Nicole was saying something about two separate groups. Did she mean...?

Then Simon spoke up, making everything clear with his traditional bluntness. "We've decided to put you both through to the next round." The girls screamed. Harry fell to his knees, overcome with relief and excitement. "This is a lifeline," Simon continued. "You've got a real shot here, guys."

It was now up to the boys to decide if they wanted

to accept this new offer. They were given just five minutes to talk it out and either agree to continue on the show as a group, or go home separately.

Backstage again, Harry couldn't hide his happiness. "It went from the worst feeling in the world to the best!" he told Dermot O'Leary, who was waiting to interview these two new boy and girl bands.

But once the party atmosphere ebbed away, the five lads found themselves wondering what came next. They were now a pop group. They just didn't have a name yet, and didn't really know each other. The next stage of filming was a few months away, but since the auditions and bootcamp footage wouldn't be aired until later they had to agree to keep what had just happened a secret. Harry reluctantly deleted his beloved Facebook account, so he wouldn't accidentally reveal anything!

"We should all meet up," said Louis, "you know, before we start filming again, get to know each other properly." They all loved that idea, but there was one problem – Niall lived in Dublin, which would make it tricky to just pop over for a night out.

"I've got an idea!" said Harry.

Soon enough, his four new bandmates followed Harry back home, where his mum and stepdad Robyn put them all up in a small bungalow at the bottom of their garden and left them to it. Of course, five teenage lads sharing a house without parents watching over their every move meant that things like cooking, cleaning and practising their singing didn't always get done!

"Who wants to play some footy?" Harry asked. They were barely ten minutes into rehearsals, but nobody complained. There'd be plenty of time for that once they were in front of the cameras, under Simon Cowell's supervision. They lived off chips and Pot Noodles for weeks, watched telly together and had a laugh.

"This is great," Louis said during one of the many late-night chats he shared with Harry, who was quickly becoming his best mate in the group. Harry agreed.

The big question hanging over them was what their band should be called. They'd been given a lot of freedom to figure out their style and vibe by themselves, and this was an important part of that process. Harry started thinking. He'd come up with White Eskimo's name, surely he could do it again? He thought back to how it felt, being put together as a group, that sudden change of direction. Wait a minute. Direction. He liked that. It felt full of purpose. And five lads had now become one unit, with a shared goal in mind. They were all headed in...

"One Direction," Harry blurted out. "I mean, what about that? For our name?"

Louis, Niall, Zayn and Liam all looked at each other. That was really good, they agreed. As easily as that, the UK's next big boy band had a name and identity all of their own. They passed the name on to the show's producers, who came back with a thumbs up. They weren't five random teenagers anymore. They were One Direction. It felt good. It felt right.

Harry had worried that being thrown together like this would create friction, especially since they'd all entered *The X Factor* dreaming of being big solo pop stars. All it would take was one little splinter of resentment from any one of them and the vibe would be ruined. Instead, they'd simply hung out together, becoming real friends rather than formal music business partners.

"You know what, I don't actually mind if we don't win *The X Factor*," Harry confessed one night through a mouthful of KFC. "This has been the best summer ever. It's been worth it just for this." The others murmured their agreement.

Of course, he did want to win – they all did – but they all understood what he meant. They had a long road ahead of them, with a lot of hard work, and no guarantee of success at the end of it. But they all agreed: it should always be this much fun.

CHAPTER 7

JUST THE BEGINNING

Harry yawned and stretched. The pilot had just announced they'd be landing in Spain soon. Everyone in the Groups category was being flown there for the next stage of *The X Factor* competition.

This was the part of the process where they'd stay in a luxury resort with one of the judges watching over them. They didn't know yet who that would be, but Harry hoped it would be Simon Cowell. Yeah, he could be absolutely brutal in his put-downs, but he also had a reputation for creating pop magic and was absolutely committed to helping his acts succeed.

The lads were driven to a sun-kissed villa, right on the coast. It was baking hot as they lined up with the other groups to meet their judge. The doors to the villa opened and – yes! – Simon Cowell walked out. He was joined by 80s pop star Sinitta, Simon's ex-girlfriend and now one of his most trusted advisors. After a cheerful greeting, everyone made their way to their accommodation. There were a lot of rehearsals and coaching to get through before Simon picked the groups he wanted to put through to the live shows.

Of course, being the youngest boy band ever featured on the show meant that keeping the 1D lads on task wasn't always easy. The lure of the beach was very strong, and they kept sneaking off for a swim.

"Aaargh!" yelped Louis during one such dip. Harry dashed over, splashing through the waves to reach his friend. The water around Louis was turning red with blood! He'd been stung by a poisonous sea urchin and was rushed to hospital. It wasn't serious, thankfully, but with their make-or-break performance for Simon only a few hours away, it could still spell disaster for the band if he wasn't released in time.

The other groups gave their performances, and there was still no sign of Louis. Harry, Liam, Zayn and Niall debated whether or not they could perform as a foursome rather than miss out completely.

They'd picked the song 'Torn' by Natalie Imbruglia, with Liam handling lead vocals at the start and Harry taking over halfway through. The others could provide harmonies, so as not to highlight Louis's absence. But then, to their relief, Louis arrived, limping but ready to perform. They smashed their acapella performance on Simon's sunny terrace. Simon gave his approval. Some of the groups went home in tears, but One Direction were headed to *The X Factor* live shows!

Back in the UK, Harry tried to get his head around normal life for a few weeks. He borrowed some money from his mum and bought loads of new clothes. It wasn't because he was suddenly full of pop star arrogance, he just knew he'd need a lot of stage outfits for what was coming!

"It's him, it's definitely him!" Harry could hear the girls whispering behind him. He'd stopped for snacks on the way down to London for the next leg of *The X Factor* experience. He turned around. The girls giggled, stared, then ran away. The audition episodes that he'd filmed back in April had just starting airing on TV, and people were starting to recognise him. It was a very weird feeling.

Before the spectacular weekly live shows began, during which the judges would hand the fate of their acts over to the voting public, all the acts had filmed visits at home. For the 1D lads, it was a lovely chance to see where each of them came from. They got mobbed by fans at Louis's old school. People lined up outside HMV for a signed poster in Zayn's hometown of Bradford. For Harry, it meant literally going home – with crowds spilling over his neighbour's gardens. Of course, his mum and stepdad already knew the boys from their summer break and welcomed them all as if they were family.

Everything that had happened since that hopeful audition in Manchester felt like a blur. But now that the country had been introduced to One Direction, and apparently gone mad for them overnight, it was like a runaway train.

The reaction to their performance on the first live episode was crazy. The second, even more so! Each week they offered their own version of a hit song, and each week the audience loved it more than ever. They still held their breath when the results of the phone votes were read out, but any anxiety quickly evaporated in the heat of their fans' adoration. One Direction were never in the bottom two acts, in danger of being voted off.

Even better, with each week they could feel themselves becoming better and better as a group. Their singing was more confident, their stage presence more energetic. They had training and coaching all the time – there was no way Simon would let them get away without that – but there was something happening inside each of them, and inside their friendship. Something was growing and getting stronger. All they could do was hang on and enjoy the ride.

It was down to just three acts now: One Direction, Rebecca Ferguson and Matt Cardle. The big final live show was going to be a spectacular event, with huge guest stars. Harry and the boys were going to be joined on stage by Robbie Williams, actual boy-band royalty! Harry was shaking with nerves when he met Robbie. Just like him, he was a normal lad from a small Northern town who wanted to be a star. Robbie had made it, so maybe he could too?

Robbie was incredibly nice and friendly. He saw a lot of himself in the young Harry, and gave him heartfelt words of encouragement. Together they sang 'She's the One', one of Robbie's big solo hits from 1999. The big sweeping ballad was a perfect match for One Direction's youthful earnestness. It felt like a torch was being passed, from one generation of pop stars to the next.

After the song had finished, Dermot asked Harry how it had felt, singing alongside Britain's most successful boy-band star. Harry, who usually clicked straight into cool mode when faced with a microphone, stumbled over his words. He could barely hear himself speak – the crowd was still screaming!

"It's incredible," he mumbled, "It's such an honour to sing with Robbie."

Backstage Harry saw Will.I.Am and Rihanna, who would be performing with Rebecca and Matt. He had to pinch himself. One minute he'd been doing his GCSEs. Now he was on live TV with the biggest names in pop, getting advice from one of his idols. He felt unbeatable.

The show was a roaring success. The phone votes closed. The boys stood nervously on stage with Simon, waiting for the verdict. Dermot announced the first act that would go through to the final: "Matt!" Harry chewed his fingernails anxiously. "The second act still in the final is..." Why did they make these pauses go on so long? "Rebecca!"

There was a split second of stunned silence from the boys. Dermot asked what the future for One Direction was now.

Simon took his microphone. "This is just the beginning for these boys." And he was right!

CHAPTER 8

X FACTOR ON THE ROAD

Backstage after placing third on *The X Factor*, the mood was mixed. The boys had hoped they could go all the way and become the first boy band to win the famous pop series. But it definitely didn't feel like they'd lost. Hundreds of thousands of fans had queued to see them or called in and texted to support them. The people wanted more One Direction, and Simon was going to make sure they got it!

He immediately signed the group to his record label, SYCO, and put plans in motion to turn them into global megastars. It was the middle of December, and almost the end of a whirlwind year.

"Go home, lads," Simon told them. "Relax and enjoy yourselves because next year, the hard work really begins."

Back in Holmes Chapel, Harry tried to treat it as just a normal Christmas but even though he lounged around on the sofa, watching old films and stuffing his face with his mum's cooking, it was clear things were not going to be normal. He'd open the curtains to see groups of excited girls waving and screaming up at him. Whenever he could, he'd take the time to pop outside to say hello, give hugs and take selfies. But it soon became clear that if he did that every single time, he'd never get to go back inside!

"This is getting a bit mad," he said to Louis during one of their many phone calls over the holiday. Liam, Zayn and Niall all confirmed they were having similar experiences over long text chats. Like most teen boys, they were thrilled by the wave of attention from starstruck girls, but it was taking a lot of getting used to!

January arrived, and Harry found himself jetting to Los Angeles with the guys for an intense week of meetings and discussions about their first album. Simon wasn't kidding when he said they'd be working hard! Harry had been to America before, on a Disney holiday as a kid, but this was completely different. Limousines, fancy hotels, skyscrapers and top restaurants!

Harry chilled out by the pool whenever he got a chance, which wasn't very often. He even bumped into fellow *X Factor* contestant Cher Lloyd, who had been eliminated just before One Direction. She was in LA for the same reason as the boys, setting up the next stage of her career. She and Harry hung out at a mall and swapped stories about their bizarre new celebrity lifestyles. It was nice to know that he wasn't alone in finding it all a bit overwhelming.

But mostly this week was all about meetings. Lots and lots of meetings. One of the most important was with Nadir Khayat, also known as RedOne. Harry had never heard of him, but this was the record producer who had crafted massive hit songs for Lady Gaga, Mariah Carey and Shakira. Then they had dinner with Max Martin, who had helped make Britney Spears a superstar. They popped into the office of Randy Jackson, one of the hosts of *American Idol*. Simon was pulling in every connection he had, and struck a deal with Sony to release One

Direction's records in the USA. Harry and friends were introduced to a small army of people who were going to help them over there – publicists, lawyers, even bodyguards! This was serious stuff!

Before their feet could even touch the ground, it was back home to the UK to take part in the *X Factor* live tour. Thirty-seven arena concerts lay ahead of them, criss-crossing the country in the company of other acts from their season of the show, including the winner Matt Cardle.

Traditionally on previous *X Factor* tours, the winner of the show got to sing five songs, with the other acts singing two. But because One Direction were already so famous, and because so many of the ticket sales were to people eager to see the boys live for the first time, they also got to perform five songs this time.

The tour was a blast, like the last day of term for the *X Factor*'s Class of 2010, with Harry and Louis quickly getting a reputation as backstage pranksters. They had multiple food fights and would challenge each other to use weird phrases like 'winkle pickers' live on stage, and then try to hide their laughter at the daft joke that only they understood. One morning Harry even woke up to discover two straws had been stuck up his nose. Louis creased up in hysterics. "You're a walrus!" he laughed.

The mucking about wasn't just off-stage. One night Louis jumped on Harry mid-performance and they ran around the stage like little kids. The fans loved their spontaneous energy. So many earlier boy bands had stuck to their rigid dance routines, so One Direction's goofy, boisterous personalities were really making them stand out.

But for all the fun they had, it was hard work. Sometimes two big shows a day for several days in a row, then off to the next city to do it all again, and again, and again. Between shows they were also taking their music seriously. They didn't want to be one of those boy bands who just did what they were told by others. They had their own ideas for songs, melodies and tunes they wanted to develop, lyrics they liked. It all got stirred into the One Direction recipe, ready for when they sat down with their producers and started putting an album together.

The *X Factor* tour finished in the middle of April,

and Harry and Louis grabbed the chance to take a holiday before plunging into recording sessions. Together with two childhood friends, they flew to France to go skiing in the Alps.

"Excusez moi, could you take a photo?" Some tourists at the resort were holding out their camera to Harry and Louis. After the last few months of madness, they were used to this by now. Harry and Louis immediately struck a pose, smiling for yet another fan photo. The tourists looked at them, confused. "No, no. You take our picture!" Harry and Louis fell about laughing. The tourists had no idea who they were. They just wanted someone to take a holiday pic for them!

"Maybe we're not that famous after all," Harry joked. It was an important lesson in humility, and Harry took it to heart as he plunged back into developing One Direction's first songs.

CHAPTER 9

ONE DIRECTION GOES GLOBAL

Simon Cowell's network had been busy finding songs for the guys, and after a lot of debate they'd all agreed that 'What Makes You Beautiful' was the perfect one to launch their career officially.

With an August release date planned, the song's upbeat power-pop sound had exactly the vibe they wanted. It was a proper anthem, a song that everyone could sing along to, with a chorus that made everyone want to jump out of their seat.

Harry also liked that while the song was about a girl, it wasn't the sort of cheesy 'ooh baby' love song that boy bands usually released. It was empowering and encouraged people to be happy with themselves. Having had so many female friends at school, who would confide in him how self-conscious they sometimes felt, he appreciated that this song tackled those insecurities in a positive way.

The group flew to Stockholm, Sweden, and got to work. Their producer, Rami, had worked with Westlife, NSYNC, Backstreet Boys and loads of other huge pop names, and the lads trusted him completely. After long, intense rehearsal and recording sessions, they flew back to the UK where they kept working on the song, then jetted over to Malibu, California, to finish it off and shoot the video.

It was non-stop, and whatever tiny gaps they had in the schedule were filled with interviews and promotions. A camera crew from ITV followed them everywhere, making a follow-up documentary to show what happened to the band after *The X Factor*. Harry had never been known for being shy, but talking about himself so often, for so long, was one of the many things that he hadn't expected. He could see how quickly and easily the celebrity life could make you arrogant and selfish. Whenever it felt too much, he'd phone his mum for a reminder that deep down he was still just Harry, a teenager from Cheshire.

'What Makes You Beautiful' was revealed to the world on the *Scott Mills Breakfast Show* on Radio 1. Harry gathered around a radio with Louis, Niall, Zayn and Liam, waiting to hear it played. Despite everything they'd been through together already, there was something amazing about knowing their song was about to be broadcast to millions of people.

The catchy intro, inspired by the song 'Summer Loving' from the musical *Grease*, blasted from the speaker and the lads couldn't contain their excitement, hugging each other and bouncing around the room. Their first single! And it was brilliant!

Fans didn't want to just hear the song, though. They wanted to see the handsome quintet performing it. The song's first live TV performance was set to take place on the ITV game show *Red or Black?* This was the big Saturday night show at the time, hosted by none other than Ant and Dec, and the announcement that One Direction would be providing the musical entertainment created a buzz among their fans.

They didn't want to just walk out on stage and sing. One Direction had got to this point by doing things differently, so plans were made to prank the audience, both in the studio and at home. When the time came for the performance, Ant and Dec pretended that the band were late. The cameras then cut to the boys running to get on a Tube train, packed with female fans, where they began singing the song. They'd then leave the London Underground and be chased by their fans all the way to the studio while the song kept playing. Finally they'd burst out onto the stage and finish the song live.

It was a great idea, playful and fun, and it summed up One Direction's personality. It was also a reference to The Beatles, who had been pursued by fans in exactly the same way in their 1960s movie *A Hard Day's Night*. Harry loved the whole concept, and threw himself into it.

However, by the time they were on stage finishing the song in front of the audience, it was clear something was wrong, and at the worst possible time. It was Harry's solo moment, he was in the spotlight all by himself, and his voice was struggling.

"Baby, you light up my world like nobody else..." he sang, but even with the microphone the audience could barely hear him. "The way that you flip your hair gets me overwhelmed..." he continued, starting to panic. He mumbled the last few words: "But when you smile at the ground, it ain't hard to tell."

He felt sick to the pit of his stomach. He looked to his bandmates with an apologetic shrug. Niall patted him on the back, reassuringly. There was no time to linger – they were still performing on live TV! – but it preyed on Harry's mind for the rest of the night. While the other lads celebrated, he sat in the dressing room, gloomily scrolling through social media, looking at all the negative reactions to his vocal stumble. Some of them were really horrible.

There and then, Harry made a choice. He'd been so caught up in everything else, he'd let the most important thing – the music – lose focus. This wouldn't be the end of the world, not even the end of the group, but this was his job now. He had to treat it like that. There'd be lots of fun, of course, but it always had to come second to putting on a good show. He gritted his teeth, put his phone away, and went to join the lads. They had the perfect pop song to promote, and he wasn't going to let them down again.

CHAPTER 10

ONE DIRECTION FEVER

'What Makes You Beautiful' was a huge hit and went straight into the charts at Number 1, becoming exactly the sort of summer-defining anthem the boys had wanted it to be. Now all the attention was on their first album. It was due to be released by the end of the year, making it the must-have record for Christmas.

Simon and his production team had sourced potential songs from dozens of songwriters. Kelly Clarkson provided a track called 'Tell Me A Lie' that she'd co-written with the intention of singing it herself, before realising it suited the 1D lads better. A couple of songs came in from Ed Sheeran and were deemed special enough to be held back as bonus tracks.

But the boys were also keen to be as involved

as possible in the songwriting process whenever possible. They felt it was important that their album had their personal stamp on it, but also – for Harry in particular – getting more experience writing and recording songs was incredibly interesting. In the end, the boys were credited as official co-writers of three of the album's songs – 'Taken', 'Everything About You' and 'Same Mistakes'.

One recording session in particular, for the song 'I Want' with writer-producer Tom Fletcher, really brought home how important this was.

"You remind me of when we were starting out," Tom told the lads, referring to his band McFly, who had a string of catchy pop-punk hits in the early 2000s. Sitting around, jamming on instruments, feeling a song come together, it all reminded Harry of being at school, rehearsing with White Eskimo at break time. He was determined to keep that authentic band spirit alive, even in this glamorous new world of polished celebrity pop.

The months flew past in a blur of concerts, TV appearances and promotional events. Harry took every opportunity to learn more about showbusiness and get advice from the celebrities he was rubbing shoulders with.

During one charity event he was sitting at the same table as Radio 1 DJ Nick Grimshaw, and the two really hit it off. Nick was ten years older than Harry, but came from the North West of England too. They shared the same sense of humour, and Harry found it really useful to see how Nick handled years of hanging out with pop stars while still keeping his feet on the ground.

The recording on the album, now called *Up All Night*, was going well, and the group's popularity just seemed to keep on rising. However, even these achievements threatened to be overshadowed by Harry's love life, which had become an obsession, not just for fans but for gossip journalists everywhere.

Harry was romantically linked with loads of famous women, often based on nothing more than a photo of them together at some event or other. Almost always, these were just friends who happened to be female – Harry had always been comfortable being friends with girls. But there was one relationship that kept coming back in the headlines.

Harry had met Caroline Flack while they were on *The X Factor*. Fifteen years older than Harry, she presented the bonus show, *The Xtra Factor*, and Harry made no secret of his crush on her. He flirted with her in person. He flirted with her on social media. And, of course, she found it hard to resist. Their friendly meet-ups gradually became more serious, and while neither of them were keen on putting an official name to their relationship status, it was clear to the world that they were more than just pals.

Harry was smitten, absolutely head over heels for this smart and talented woman, but the intense scrutiny was very hard to deal with. Sometimes it could be fun – firing off a cheeky tweet that sent the gossip pages into a frenzy – but it also made it incredibly difficult to build any kind of normal relationship.

Unlike boy bands before them, who were often forced by their managers to keep their romantic life a secret in case it broke the spell they had cast over their fans, One Direction decided from the start that they wouldn't hide their love lives. It was great knowing that he wouldn't have to sneak around and lie about who he was seeing, but that openness also created problems for Harry.

Between Caroline's TV commitments and Harry's constant recording and performing, there were precious few moments they could spend together to figure out what exactly was happening between them. Any time they did appear in public together, it was in the glare of dozens of camera flashes.

Love was far from the only thing on Harry's mind. *Up All Night* was finally released in the UK on 21 November 2011. It debuted in the chart in second place, but was the fastest selling album of the entire year. Throughout the month it rolled out in other countries, but not everywhere. The big USA release wouldn't happen until the Spring of 2012, when the band would be available to fly over and promote it in person.

Having the album out there felt good. The sales were fantastic, of course, but Harry was pleased at just how good the reviews were. Boy bands didn't usually get the best critical reception and, given their young age, he'd been expecting some pretty mean comments from the music magazines and websites.

There were some snooty reviews, but also plenty more that appreciated just what a diverse, confident collection of pop songs *Up All Night* offered. That credibility was important to Harry, who wanted 1D to be seen as more than just five handsome faces dancing to other people's music.

The crunch came during the recording of the next season of *The X Factor*. One Direction were brought back several times to perform on the show as guests, which gave Harry and Caroline a good excuse to get together, as she'd returned to host *The Xtra Factor*. When the time came for the live finals in December – which only a year ago had seen Harry and friends quaking on stage, being told they'd been outvoted – the word came down from on high that Harry and Caroline were to keep clear of each other during the show. Their relationship was taking media attention away from the new acts, with girl group Little Mix finally breaking the tradition and becoming the first non-solo act to win.

The romance was distracting in more serious ways as well. All the 1D boys had attracted hardcore fans who were obsessed with their chosen favourite, but Harry seemed to get it the worst. Girls who were pulled up on stage during their shows for Harry to serenade would receive nasty social media messages once fans found out who they were. Caroline got it even worse, facing vile online abuse every day from fans who thought she was 'stealing' Harry from them. They'd send cruel messages about her age, about her looks, about anything that might hurt her, while unofficial fan magazines ran hate articles about her. Harry was mortified. This was a dark side to fame that he'd never really thought about, and it was painful to experience for real. It was an impossible situation. Caroline couldn't leave her home without being mobbed by photographers, much to her neighbours' annoyance.

"I need some space," Caroline told Harry as she took off to India for a month-long holiday with her mates. When she got back, they continued to meet up, but it was clear that no matter what their feelings for one another were, there was no future in a relationship that would always take place under such a fierce media microscope. Sadly, reluctantly, they agreed to part ways – and finally put all the speculation to rest.

It was 27 January 2012 when Harry broke the news, pleading on social media for people to respect Caroline's privacy and leave her alone. He was heartbroken, but also worried about what this would mean for any future relationships. For someone as friendly and flirty as Harry, knowing that just being seen with a girl could bring an avalanche of abuse into their lives was a troubling thought.

The American launch of *Up All Night* was only weeks away, and his life was about to take another massive turn.

CHAPTER 11

BRUSHING SHOULDERS WITH THE STARS

Harry made himself comfortable on the massage table. The rest of the band had treated him to a spa treatment at their latest hotel to mark his eighteenth birthday on 1 February. He smiled to himself, happy to have such good friends around him for an important milestone in his life. He was so lost in thought that he didn't even notice the masseur had stepped away, and Louis, Niall, Liam and Zayn had crept in with buckets of ice cold water.

SPLOSH!

Harry shrieked in surprise, but his screams quickly turned to laughter as he saw the others falling about in hysterics at their successful prank. This was the sort of silliness that they used to keep each other sane during all their travelling. Harry vowed to get revenge, but secretly he loved it. That was a good thing, as they were about to spend a lot more time in America, where just getting from one city to another could take all day.

It was a crisp spring morning in New York on 10 March 2012 as Harry and the boys were sitting on a specially branded London bus, bright red with the One Direction logo on the side. There would be no pranks on this journey. In a few minutes it would take them through the streets of Manhattan to the Rockefeller Centre, a huge space flanked by skyscrapers where they'd make their live debut on American TV as part of the *Today* show.

Harry tried to mask his nerves as the bus set off. The lads dutifully climbed to the open-air top deck to wave to their fans along the way. And even though they hadn't even released a single in America yet, they did have fans. Lots of them. And around 15,000 of them were now waiting to see them, some having camped out overnight on the street to bag the perfect spot.

Harry thought back to the meeting in which their

US promoters had explained their bold approach to marketing One Direction to American audiences. Other British boy bands had struggled to break into American pop. Even Take That, one of the biggest pop acts in the UK, had only ever scored one hit single in America.

One Direction had a big advantage, their US team had said. They had social media. In 2012, Twitter was still only a few years old, Facebook was huge, YouTube was taking off. That was where young pop fans were looking for their next obsession. So rather than begging US radio stations to pick up 'What Makes You Beautiful', and hoping for the best, they flipped it around.

Using social media posts, they encouraged 1D's few thousands fans to bombard their local radio stations asking them to play the song. They could enter contests to win a One Direction concert in their town. Simon Cowell hired a special marketing agency to run an online mystery in which fans had to help One Direction find a stolen laptop containing their songs.

The 1D Facebook page went from 4,000 US fans

to 40,000 in a matter of weeks. The album launch was brought forward from the end of March to the middle of the month, as demand reached fever pitch. The promotion was intense. The boys supported the American boy band Big Time Rush on their tour, and even guest starred on *iCarly*. Simon did anything and everything that might put Harry, Liam, Louis, Niall and Zayn in front of American tweens.

By the time *Up All Night*'s release date arrived, DJs were begging the record company for a copy of this record everyone kept asking about, and venues were scrambling to book what looked like the biggest new band of the year!

Wearing coordinated combinations of red, blue and grey clothes, Harry and the boys stood on a bright white stage in the middle of the street. The hosts of the *Today* show quizzed them on what they liked most about American girls.

"They're loud!" joked Niall, quick as a flash, and the crowd screamed at ear-splitting volume right on cue. They performed three songs – 'What Makes You Beautiful', 'More than This', and 'One Thing' – and left the crowd cheering for more.

Up All Night was released the following day across America and went straight to the top of the Billboard chart. This was a huge achievement. America hadn't had a chart-topping album from a boy band since *NSYNC's *Celebrity* eleven years earlier! Even more impressive was the fact that no British band had ever gone straight to the top of the US album chart with their first record. Harry was stunned. Not only were they the biggest band in the USA, but they were also Guinness World Record breakers!

This success wasn't going to be allowed to fizzle out. The boys' schedule for the next month was punishing. As well as interviews, shows and photo opportunities, there were even more high-profile TV appearances to squeeze in.

In early April, they'd be appearing on the legendary comedy show *Saturday Night Live*. Not only would that involve performing two songs – 'What Makes You Beautiful' and 'One Thing' – but they'd also have to take part in a comedy sketch with Sofía Vergara, star of the hit sitcom *Modern Family*.

The thought of it made Harry's stomach do loop-the-loops. Singing live on TV was one thing, but comedy? He'd enjoyed filming his cameo for *iCarly* with Miranda Cosgrove and Jennette McCurdy, but he'd been able to try different takes with the director helping him get it right. Live comedy? On a late-night show for adults? It was a terrifying prospect, but also an exciting one. Music was his first love, but the idea of acting had always appealed to him. What better way to give it a try than on the most famous comedy show in the world, with tens of millions of American viewers watching?

Before then, the lads were due to perform at Nickelodeon's Kids Choice Awards, a huge event featuring some of the biggest stars on the planet. Will Smith was the host! Robert Downey Jr was there, along with Zac Efron and Michelle Obama – the First Lady of the United States! Backstage, in the maze of corridors under the Los Angeles arena where it was taking place, a familiar voice rang out:

"You're so cute! I love you!" It was Katy Perry! The boys were starstruck. Harry couldn't help wondering, did she know they'd namechecked her on 'Up All Night'?

The boys performed two songs to the screaming

crowd, emerging from glowing boxes to an incredible response. They bopped through 'What Makes You Beautiful', already shaping up to be a summer hit in the US like it had been back home the year before. Fans waved homemade banners declaring their love for One Direction.

As they sang, Harry noticed someone in particular in the crowd. Dancing away to their performance was none other than Taylor Swift! She was there with her friend Selena Gomez, and Harry could see they were whispering to each other and giggling while watching the performance. After the show, Harry and Taylor were introduced to each other. They chatted and swapped phone numbers. Harry's heart was racing. He was flirting with one of the most famous and beautiful women in the world! And, best of all, she seemed to be into it!

That same week, Justin Bieber invited the 1D boys and Taylor to come and hang out at his LA mansion. It was clear to everyone that there were sparks between Harry and Taylor. Liam, Niall, Zayn and Louis couldn't help teasing their friend about it. Even Justin got involved, talking with Taylor and reporting back that she definitely thought one of the boys was hot. But who was it? Harry hoped he knew the answer!

CHAPTER 12

MAKE HAY WHILE THE SUN SHINES

The summer of 2012 was a whirlwind for Harry. Concerts across America had to be fitted around recording sessions for One Direction's second album. He'd treated himself to a motorbike to celebrate adulthood and could often be seen riding it around the glamorous parts of Los Angeles.

Harry was also starting to think more seriously about what to do with the enormous amount of money he was earning. As much as he loved living and working in America, he knew that he wanted to keep his roots in the UK and splashed out on a house in London's leafy Hampstead Heath for a cool five million pounds. He tried to work out how long it would have taken to save up that much working at the bakery in Holmes Chapel, but quickly lost count!

The success of *Up All Night* in America meant that Simon had been able to weave his special kind of business magic on the follow-up. Producers and songwriters were now fighting for the chance to contribute a track to a One Direction album. The boys weren't in a rush to change a winning formula though. Rami Yacoub and his Swedish studio were trusted to work on most of the tracks, while friends like Ed Sheeran and McFly's Tom Fletcher were asked back to work on more songs.

The 1D lads were more involved in the writing this time as well, co-writing three of the tracks on the album – 'Last First Kiss', 'Back For You', and 'Summer Love' – as well as two bonus tracks: 'Irresistible' and 'Still the One'. This was the part Harry really loved. Performing on stage was great, and still gave him a huge buzz, but actually being involved in putting a song together felt like he was learning new skills and getting experience that would come in useful for years to come.

Recording the album, now called *Take Me Home*, meant flying between Sweden, California and London while also continuing to promote *Up All Night* in America. None of the boys complained. At least not for long. They'd seen enough examples from previous groups. All five of them knew that boy bands usually burned brightly for a short time, so committing to a new album every year for as long as they could made sense. 'Make hay while the sun shines' was the phrase that came to mind, meaning you should grab as much good fortune as you could while it lasted.

That belief was also reflected in the song they all agreed would be the album's first single. 'Live While We're Young' was another uplifting anthem with lyrics about seizing the moment. It was also a track that put Zayn in the spotlight, with him singing most of the verses, something that Harry was particularly pleased about.

As preparations were made for the launch of *Take Me Home*, the American record company had called a meeting with the band to discuss a delicate matter. The company executives explained that they wanted to push Harry as the 'face' of One Direction, as previous successful boy bands had always featured one member who stood out from the others, like Justin Timberlake in *NSYNC. With his voice, looks and personality they reckoned Harry fitted the bill. But Harry shut them down straight away. One Direction wasn't going to be like other boy bands. It was the key to why the band even existed in the first place. Simon had seen five talented but unpolished performers who would work better as a team than on their own, and it had paid off. Harry had no desire to ruin that balance, and the other lads backed him up. They were all equal and that was how it would stay.

'Live While We're Young' was released at the end of September and was an instant smash. The video clocked up over eight million views on YouTube in its first day, while the single itself landed in Top 10s all over the world. It entered the US charts at number 3, the first single by a British act to debut that high in America since Elton John's 'Candle in the Wind' fifteen years earlier! The song was used in the Pepsi Superbowl commercial, with Harry pretending that NFL star Drew Brees was joining the group. It even featured in the Thanksgiving episode of hit TV show *Glee*, the second time the show had featured cast members covering 1D.

With two hit albums to their name, One Direction was now firmly established as a big deal in America. More awards ceremonies followed, including big wins at MTV's Video Music Awards, which are like the Oscars for pop music. All five members were being invited to everything from fashion shows to sporting events, as everybody tried to add a little 1D sizzle to their guest lists.

In early November, Harry met up with Taylor Swift. Both she and One Direction were due to perform on the US version of *The X Factor*. They'd not seen each other since earlier in the year, when their budding romance had been put on pause. Harry dated supermodel Cara Delevingne in between, while Taylor had dated Conor Kennedy, a member of one of America's most influential political families.

Those old sparks fired up again as soon as they saw each other. *The X Factor*'s host, former *Saved By The Bell* star Mario Lopez, tweeted that he'd seen Harry and Taylor holding hands backstage. Before long, other people were reporting that they'd seen the couple together, staying at the same hotels, riding in the same cars. Once again, Harry was at the centre of a gossip hurricane.

Harry and Taylor — or 'Haylor' as fans quickly dubbed their relationship — went public on 2 December, when they were photographed sharing a romantic walk around Central Park Zoo in New York.

Taylor then joined Harry on a trip home, leading to the bizarre sight of two of the most famous people in the world having a Christmas pub lunch together in Cheshire! Taylor even spent her twenty-third birthday in England with Harry. Always a romantic, he phoned a local cake shop and begged them to make some special cupcakes for her!

They were back in New York for New Year's Eve, where Taylor was performing in Times Square as part of the traditional live TV countdown, and then jetted off together for a sunny Caribbean holiday to start 2013.

Suddenly, sadly, it all went wrong. They had a big argument, and Taylor was photographed leaving on a boat, by herself. Their romance had only lasted a few months, but it had generated hundreds of headlines, and Taylor's fans would spend years trying to work out which of her songs and performances were about this tumultuous affair.

For Harry, it was a kind of heartbreak that was starting to feel quite familiar. He'd been burned twice now by trying to build a relationship in the glare of media attention, and both times it hadn't worked out. Maybe it was for the best. The One Direction rollercoaster was still travelling at top speed, and he'd need all his energy to hold on.

CHAPTER 13

AROUND THE WORLD

Still emotionally bruised from the very public Taylor breakup, Harry entered 2013 knowing almost exactly how it would go. When he'd been nervously queuing outside *The X Factor* auditions in Manchester, still a schoolboy, the idea that within just a few years he'd be used to global fame would have seemed unbelievable. And yet here he was.

At the end of February, One Direction would set off on their next tour. They'd travel across the UK, Europe, the USA, Australia and Asia supporting *Take Me Home*, which was already on track to outsell *Up All Night* by millions of copies. In the brief gaps between shows, they'd do hundreds of interviews and TV appearances. Somehow, somewhere, they'd find time to get in the studio and work on their third album, which was already scheduled to release in November.

It was all mapped out, and while Harry found some comfort in the predictability, it was also starting to become a little frustrating. All five 1D members had signed a contract immediately after *The X Factor*, which covered their first two albums. They'd now signed a new contract which ensured at least three more albums.

There was also a financial bonus written into the deal, which meant they'd all get extra money provided they stayed together as a five-piece group for the duration of the contract. This was included to avoid the problems that earlier boy bands had faced, when members would leave to go solo. None of the boys had minded that at the time – they all wanted to stick together – but as years of relentless touring and recording stretched out before him, Harry couldn't help feeling a bit suffocated by it all.

There were things about being famous that he absolutely loved. Seeing so many different places around the world, meeting and collaborating with some incredibly creative and successful people. These were the things he'd always wanted, and he was thrilled that he got to do them.

But there were also things that brought his teenage anxiety creeping back. Interviews were hard. A natural people-pleaser, he wanted journalists to come away from meeting the group with the quotes and insights they were looking for. As the band went from being cute boys to young men, those questions were becoming more and more intrusive.

He'd be asked about his love life in ways that left him feeling deeply uncomfortable, and inside he'd be incredibly stressed about saying the wrong thing. For all the pranks and mucking about the lads got up to, their contracts had quite strict rules about maintaining a clean image for their young fans. Balancing that with the more adult questions they were now getting worried him a lot.

The same was true on social media. From the start, all five had insisted they wanted to run their own social accounts so they could interact authentically with fans. Their record label had offered to hire people to post on their behalf, but that just felt too weird. As the public scrutiny became more and more intense, Harry found himself posting less and less. Zayn had already sparked headlines when he'd got involved in a Twitter argument with members of rival boy band The Wanted, and Harry fretted that he'd post the wrong thing and cause a similar blow-up.

All of these thoughts were swirling around his head as they kicked off the 'Take Me Home' tour in London at the end of February, to a screaming home audience. All doubts and worries evaporated in that moment. If being in One Direction was starting to feel a lot like a job, at least it was the best job in the world! The tour took them all over the UK and Ireland for the next few months, before returning to the O2 Arena in London for the first week of April with five back-to-back concerts with only one day off!

The group were accompanied for these London shows by American film director Morgan Spurlock, who had made the Oscar-nominated fast food documentary *Super Size Me*. He was shooting the first official One Direction movie, *This Is Us*, which would combine backstage scenes and candid home movies with up-close concert footage, all in 3D! Harry was no stranger to being filmed and photographed, but having the same camera crew follow them everywhere for such a long time reminded him of being on *The X Factor*, where every moment was recorded.

One thing that helped to keep the shows feeling fresh, even as they performed the same songs every night, was sprinkling in fun cover versions. The lads would pick songs they loved, or just songs the audience wouldn't expect, and give them a 1D makeover.

But they also covered big ballads from the 90s, such as 'I Will Always Love You', made famous by Whitney Houston in 1992, or Celine Dion's 'My Heart Will Go On', a huge hit in 1997. For Harry, the best reaction was when they rapped the theme tune to Will Smith's sitcom *The Fresh Prince of Bel Air* in Dublin. The pop punk of 'Teenage Dirtbag' by Wheatus was another popular one, and very much in line with the rockier sound they were developing for their third album.

While the boys had contributed to songs on their first two albums, the third – now called *Midnight Memories* – saw them really take the songwriting side seriously. Rather than being credited together as writers, they now started working individually with different producers to bring their own specific voices to the album. Of the songs the boys worked on, only the single 'Story of My Life', credited them all as co-writers.

Liam and Louis helped to write 'Diana', 'Little Black Dress', 'Little White Lies', 'Better Than Words', and the title track, 'Midnight Memories'. Niall co-wrote 'Don't Forget Where You Belong'. Harry worked with Louis and Liam on the song 'Right Now', but was most excited about 'Something Great', a track he wrote with Gary Lightbody of indie rock band Snow Patrol. Although it was written for all of One Direction to perform, it was the first song he'd written without the other four. Rather than just being a pop star, it made him feel like a musician.

Meanwhile, the tour rumbled on. It was particularly exciting to head to Japan for two dates in November, especially as their support act there was Olly Murs. Olly had built a successful music career after being a runner-up on *The X Factor* the year before Harry and the others, and had become a good friend of the guys over the last few years.

Midnight Memories came out only a few weeks after they got home from Japan. They'd already released the lead single from the album, 'Best Song Ever', in the summer and made it part of their set list on tour. 'Story Of My Life' followed in October, and was another hit, so they knew they had at least two bangers on the record!

What would people make of the group's evolving sound though? The boys nervously waited for the first reviews and sales figures to arrive. Some critics applauded the more mature lyrics and the shift away from bubblegum pop. Other reviews sniffily declared they had lost their appeal. What really mattered was what the fans thought, and they gave the album a massive thumbs up!

Even though there were only 36 days left in the year when it launched, *Midnight Memories* still became the best-selling album of 2013 in the UK as over 685,000 fans rushed to buy it. It also entered the US album charts in the top spot, making One Direction the first band in history to have their first three albums all debut at number one.

One Direction was still on top of the world, but as the saying goes: all good things must come to an end, and 2014 would be a difficult year filled with tough, painful decisions...

CHAPTER 14

AND THEN THERE WERE FOUR

In a studio in London, all five members of One Direction were deep in discussion. It was late 2014, and they were coming to the end of yet another massive world tour. They'd played more than 60 shows in six months, filling stadiums on their most successful tour yet. Now they were finishing off their fourth album, which had to be released in just a few months' time. This wasn't the topic of conversation though.

Harry chose his words carefully. "I just think it wouldn't be a bad idea to take a break," he said. The reaction from the others was mixed. They were contracted for one more album after this one, which meant the time had come to decide if they were going to sign up for more One Direction after that. Harry had decided he wasn't going to sign. At least not yet.

It hadn't been an easy decision to make, but throughout 2013 and 2014 he'd felt the gap between what he wanted to do and what One Direction involved was getting larger. His trademark hair, once a floppy teen fringe, was now shoulder length. He'd started getting more and more tattoos. He'd looked back at photos from those first few years in the band and cringed at his style, or rather his lack of it.

Over the last year he'd started experimenting more with what he wore. Out went hoodies and jeans, in came increasingly flamboyant suits and brightly-coloured velvet, the sort of thing the rock icons of the past had worn. Musically, too, he'd been exposed to a whole new world of creative satisfaction, collaborating closely with experienced writers on his own, penning tracks for stars like Ariana Grande. Harry Styles, the person, no longer matched up with what people expected from Harry Styles, member of One Direction.

And he knew he wasn't alone in feeling this. There'd been no major arguments or bust-ups, but the dynamic within the group had shifted. How could it not, after four years living and working together every single day? Liam looked exhausted. Zayn was distant and clearly hurt to have been the only member not to get a writing credit on *Midnight Memories*. But Louis was angry.

"Things are going great," he argued. "Why would we stop now?"

"I'm not saying we should stop right now," Harry explained. "But next year, after another tour, another album? It's not just us who'll be worn out. The fans are going to start getting sick of us. What we've got is so special, but we'll lose that if we just keep touring and recording for the sake of it. We can hit pause on One Direction without ending it forever. I think that'd be healthy for everyone. I know it's what I need."

There was no easy resolution to the argument. They'd said right at the very start that when it stopped being fun, it would be time to reconsider. Maybe that time was fast approaching, if it wasn't already here. For now, they went back to finishing off the next album. Niall had suggested the title *Four*, because it was their fourth release and they'd been together for four years.

Four went on sale in November. The lads flew to Florida to promote the launch, which was when the problems started. Zayn didn't turn up for a live TV interview on the first day. He was absent for the interviews on the second day. It was only on the third day of the press tour that he joined the rest of the band. Journalists were speculating wildly about the reasons for this strange and unexpected rift, and while the band and their managers tried to explain it away, it was clear something serious was happening.

The album debuted in the number one spot, continuing the group's record-breaking run, and was one of the biggest releases of the year. Beneath the celebrations, however, there were signs that Harry's concerns about exhausting their fans might be correct. Until now, each One Direction album had sold more than the one before it. One year earlier, *Midnight Memories* had topped the US album charts by selling 546,000 copies in its first week. In comparison, *Four* had only sold 387,000 copies. For whatever reason, over 150,000 1D fans had not rushed out to buy this one.

The tour for the album was called the 'On the Road Again' tour, a name that seemed to sum up how the band were feeling about spending another year bouncing between planes and hotels, rarely seeing friends and family. It kicked off in Australia in February 2015, but from the start the guys could tell that the vibes were all wrong. Ticket sales for the Australia concerts were low, with some of the stadiums only half full.

A few weeks later, Zayn stopped performing with the band after a gig in Hong Kong. The fans and press were told that he'd had to take time off for health reasons, but behind the scenes they were taking frantic meetings to keep him on the tour. It didn't work.

"My life with One Direction has been more than I could ever have imagined," Zayn posted on 25 March. "But, after five years, I feel like it is now the right time for me to leave the band. I'd like to apologise to the fans if I've let anyone down, but I have to do what feels right in my heart. I am leaving because I want to be a normal 22-year-old who is able to relax and have some private time out of the spotlight. I know I have four friends for life in Louis, Liam, Harry and Niall. I know they will continue to be the best band in the world."

"What's that famous showbiz saying?" Harry thought to himself. "The show must go on?" He took to the stage that night in Jakarta, Indonesia, overcome with emotion. Although he'd also been considering his future in One Direction, Zayn's sudden and dramatic departure had taken him off guard. After years of doing this together, to be taking the stage without Zayn, knowing he wasn't coming back... it was too much. Harry looked at the spot where Zayn should have been standing. In the glare of the lights, the tears started to flow and Harry hurriedly wiped them away. He had to focus on getting through this performance and show that – for now at least – One Direction was still going strong.

"One more tour, one more album, then we'll see," said Harry after the show. Even Louis, the one most keen on sticking together, had to agree that they needed time to figure things out. Right now, though, they had to work out how to keep things moving with only four members. Their latest album title seemed to have been an ominous prediction...

CHAPTER 15

ONE LAST SONG

Finishing the 'On the Road Again' tour was hard, but writing and recording the first One Direction album as a foursome was surprisingly easy. Harry, Liam, Niall and even Louis had all made their peace with the idea that this would be the last 1D album for a while. Once they'd accepted it was time to take a break, the uncertainty disappeared and they attacked the task of polishing off a new collection of songs with a fresh sense of focus. More than anything, they wanted to leave the fans with a strong and positive album, not something that felt like it had been made reluctantly.

Louis was still hurting though. In May, barely two months after Zayn's exit from the group, he got into a heated Twitter argument with Naughty Boy, a rap producer who had been secretly recording music with Zayn while he was still in One Direction.

"Just leave it," Harry insisted. It would only make Naughty Boy more famous by arguing with him and the band had bigger and better things to do. Harry's relationship with social media had been strained by the endless speculation about his love life and the treatment of his girlfriends. He didn't like the negative attention that the drama created. Louis understood, but shaking the feeling of betrayal was hard.

The first single from the album, 'Drag Me Down', was released on 31 July. Eager to bring back the sense of excitement that accompanied their first songs, the band didn't announce or hype the single at all. They just released it, unannounced, and watched as fans went crazy at the surprise. It went straight to number one in the UK and delivered their biggest single week of sales ever in the US. If there had been any doubt that the fans were sticking with the boys, through all the drama, here was the proof: One Direction were still beloved.

One month later, with the single dropping back

down the charts, they dropped the news: One Direction were taking a break. Harry anxiously waited to see what the reaction would be. He knew they were about to break millions of hearts, and it wasn't a nice feeling. As necessary as it felt, he couldn't help picturing the hundreds of thousands of excited fans who had followed them over the years. "I'm sorry," he whispered to himself.

Social media and news sites lit up as word of One Direction's end spread. Except they'd been very careful not to make it sound too final in their official announcement. An 'extended hiatus' is how they'd phrased it, choosing the words deliberately to make it clear this wasn't a band splitting up, just four people taking time out to do things for themselves. They'd be gone for at least a year, but who knows? Maybe they'd be back together, re-energised and ready to carry on.

The album, *Made in the A.M.*, launched in November. Fans knew this would be the last they'd hear from the lads for some time, perhaps forever, and they pored over the lyrics looking for clues and references to the end of the group. The song 'Love

You Goodbye', written by Louis, seemed particularly meaningful now.

Although the chorus made it clear it was a song about breaking up with a girl, fans couldn't help finding deeper meaning in lines such as "It's inevitable, everything that's good comes to an end, it's impossible to know if after this we can still be friends", and "Unforgettable together, held the whole world in our hands".

There was no tour to support this album. Now that it was delivered, Harry and the others were finished with their contract. Their last show together would take place as part of the live TV broadcast *Dick Clark's New Year's Rockin' Eve* in New York's Times Square. It was a show headlined last time by Taylor Swift, with Harry watching from the sidelines. This year, he'd jetted in to headline from the Caribbean. He had been taking a holiday with Kendall Jenner, another beautiful famous woman whose close friendship with Harry seemed to be turning romantic.

It was only a short set, just three songs, all from the new album. There would be no greatest hits, no final performance of 'What Makes You Beautiful', the song that was still their most popular and enduring smash. It was a surprisingly intimate show. The set was bare and basic, the stage was small. Their arena and stadium shows had kept the audience further away, behind security barriers. Here the crowd was packed close to the front. Even the lads were dressed down. Harry had opted for a simple black hoodie, unlike the increasingly stylish costumes he'd been flaunting on tour.

"This is the best way to go out," Harry said to Liam, Niall and Louis as they prepared to perform together one last time. They agreed and hugged one another. This was One Direction stripped back to the essentials. They might have been one of the biggest musical acts in the world, but for tonight it was just four mates, loving the music, loving each other, loving the fans.

They sang 'Drag Me Down' and 'Perfect', and closed with the incredibly appropriate 'History'. The crowd screamed adoringly as Harry began to sing. "Keep getting the feelin', you wanna leave this all behind..."

Backstage, emotions ran high. There were tears and laughter, and a sense of relief as all four realised they were now free to do whatever they wanted. They huddled up, foreheads pressed together. For a split second, surrounded by best friends who had shared an incredible five-year journey together, Harry felt doubt. Was this really what he wanted? To leave this all behind?

The crowd began to chant the countdown to midnight. Ten! Nine! Eight! Seven! Six!

No, this was right. Harry felt a peace unlike anything he'd experienced before. In a few seconds it would be a new year, a new start. He was bubbling with energy and ideas for what could come next.

Five! Four! Three! Two!

Harry looked at his former bandmates and smiled.

One!

Cheers filled the air. Fireworks exploded overhead. The future had arrived. It was time for the world to meet the real Harry Styles.

CHAPTER 16

MEET HARRY

Harry flew back to the Caribbean after the New Year show with a new sense of purpose. He'd spent the last few years in One Direction networking with music industry people, learning from producers and songwriters, trying to prepare as much as possible for the day when he'd have to fly solo. That day was here, and it was a lot to take in.

Relaxing under the blazing sun on a yacht with Kendall helped. She was easy to hang out with, and they vibed together really well. Neither was sure whether this was a boyfriend-girlfriend thing yet, but Harry knew that being around her put him in a good place, mentally and emotionally. The ideas flowed when she was around, and no problem felt like it couldn't be beaten.

Zayn had already announced he'd signed a solo record deal. His first single was due at the end of January. Harry knew that Niall, Liam and Louis would also be lining up their own post-1D careers. Of course, he'd been thinking about his next move as well. But it all felt a little...weird.

"It's like we're all back on *The X Factor*," he said to Kendall as they sipped cold drinks in the shade. "We were competing against each other, then we got put together, and now we're competing again."

"It's only a competition if you treat it like one," she replied. "The fans will follow their favourites, yeah, but there's loads of people who'll listen to a Harry Styles song who maybe wouldn't have listened to a boy band. Concentrate on them, not the past."

Harry nodded and took another sip. The gentle lapping of the sea against the boat was relaxing. Zayn had been taking digs at One Direction in interviews recently, trying to distance himself from the group in order to be taken more seriously. Harry wondered if the others might do the same, if he'd be left behind as a has-been pop star while they all forged ahead with a new style. Kendall touched his hand gently and gave him a smile. He knew immediately what she meant without her having to say it. There'd be plenty of time to worry about this stuff later. For now, a clear mind and fun times were what was needed.

Once back home, Harry got in touch with a friend called Jeff Azoff. They'd first met several years earlier, during one of One Direction's concerts in Toronto, Canada. Jeff's dad was one of the most influential music executives in the world, and Jeff was working as an agent at CAA, the talent agency that handled One Direction in the USA. Although he was almost ten years older than Harry, the pair hit it off, becoming close friends. Jeff would sometimes join 1D on tour for short periods to hang out with Harry. With his family background in the industry, Harry turned to him often for advice.

Now, however, he wanted more than advice. He wanted Jeff to become his manager. This would mean him leaving his job at CAA and setting up his own company. Since Harry was one of the most famous performers in the world, and everyone was eagerly waiting to see what he'd do as a solo artist, Jeff took the plunge alongside his pal. He set up a new company, Full Stop Management, and signed Harry as a client. Meanwhile, Harry was moving into the business side of things himself. Columbia Records, the huge music label that had distributed One Direction's albums in America, had been begging him to go solo with them for years. Now that he was on the market, they snapped him up.

But Harry had learned a thing or two from his old mentor, Simon Cowell, and instead created his own record label, Erskine Records. This meant that Columbia would have to license the right to sell his albums, while he owned the music. A lot of the financial stuff and numbers made his head spin, but he took it very seriously. He'd heard too many horror stories of naïve artists being left penniless after signing the wrong deal, and he wasn't going to let that happen to him.

He was being creative as well as looking at contracts and spreadsheets. He already had a bunch of good songs lined up and planned to spend the autumn concentrating on writing more and then picking the best ones for his first solo release. Zayn's first single, 'Pillowtalk', had hit number one in the UK and USA, so the pressure was on for all the 1D boys to prove they had what it took to stay in the public eye.

Before then, Harry had to do something he'd never done before: act in a movie! His experiences on *iCarly* and *Saturday Night Live*, as well as shooting all of One Direction's videos, had got him curious about doing more acting.

"Be careful," Jeff had said. "Don't let it overshadow the music."

Harry was confident it would be OK. It was only a small part, and lots of his favourite singers, like David Bowie, had appeared in movies without losing focus.

The film was called *Dunkirk* and would be an ambitious restaging of the World War II operation that saw hundreds of stranded British soldiers rescued from the beaches of France. The story would cut between lots of different characters, from the high-up commanders to ordinary soldiers. Harry was going to play one of those, after his audition with director Christopher Nolan went well. Also in the film would be legendary actors like Kenneth Branagh and Tom Hardy.

He remembered the audition with a smile. Nolan had seen thousands of young men for the part of Alex, but felt Harry had the charm and innocence needed to make it work.

"I understand you're a singer?" the director had asked him. Of course, serious Oscar-winning directors probably didn't need to pay much attention to the pop charts or boy band magazines, but Harry liked that. It meant he'd won the role in a serious epic movie on the merits of his acting, rather than being cast in a romantic comedy because of his celebrity. Filming took place on the real beach where the rescue had taken place, and then it was back to reality to whip that all-important album into shape.

CHAPTER 17

MUSIC I WANT TO MAKE

Harry returned from filming *Dunkirk* and flew straight out again. This time he wasn't holidaying. He was about to embark on the most important two months of work in his life so far.

"I need to get out of London and LA," he'd told Jeff Azoff, now his manager.

"I know just the place," replied Jeff, and booked out the GeeJam Studios in Port Antonio, Jamaica, for the next two months.

Harry had already picked producer Jeff Bhasker to work on his debut album. Bhasker had worked with Kanye West, Beyonce, Lana Del Rey and loads of other huge artists. When Harry made contact with him, he was fresh from producing Mark Ronson's enormous hit 'Uptown Funk'.

What Harry liked wasn't just that all of Bhasker's productions had been successful, but that each one had been so different. He was a producer who understood how to develop and showcase a performer's unique voice. More than chart success, that was what Harry desperately wanted to do. Who was he going to be as an artist? Jeff could help him figure that out.

Bhasker put Harry together with musicians he knew and trusted. Alex Salibian and Tyler Johnson would co-produce as well as be playing on the album. The musical sound would be fleshed out by bassist Ryan Nasci and Mitch Rowland, an amazing guitarist who was still working in a pizza restaurant when recording began!

This wasn't the sort of set-up Harry had been used to in One Direction. While he'd helped to write songs for their albums, it was always a rushed process. He'd hand over lyrics, an idea for a melody, but then it would be taken care of by someone else while he got back to touring, interviews and all the other requirements of being in a hit boy band.

Harry was incredibly proud of the 1D songs he'd worked on, especially 'Olivia', 'Stockholm Syndrome', and 'Happily'. Those were the ones where he could feel the first flicker of the sort of songs he wanted to write. There just wasn't any time for him to really work on them as part of the One Direction machine. In Jamaica, that all changed.

"What's the rush?" Bhasker would tell him, as Harry was still in boy-band mode when it came to production. There was no yearly album deadline to hit now. "Take your time," Bhasker advised. "Let the songs come to you in their own time."

This way of working was a revelation for Harry. They would swim in the private cove near the studio, then come back and just... play music. Working with the same band, day after day, feeling their way through each idea, sharing and developing songs naturally, it lit up Harry's creativity like nothing he'd ever experienced. By night they'd unwind by watching back-to-back romantic comedies on the giant TV until they fell asleep.

Harry's vision for what the album would be gradually came into focus. He knew he wanted to draw from the singer-songwriters of the 60s and 70s that he'd grown up listening to with his dad. But he also wanted it to still feel modern and poppy, like the songs he'd sing along to in the car with his mum. More than anything, he wanted the songs to be meaningful and personal.

"There's no point doing this if it's just cheesy love songs that anyone could have written," he told Mitch, the guitarist, during one of their late-night movie marathons.

One of the first songs to fall into place was 'Sign of the Times', which would eventually become the lead single from the album. A slower, piano-led tune, Harry had written the lyrics not as a boy singing to a girl he loved, as was usually the case in One Direction. Instead he'd imagined himself as a mother who had just given birth, but who was now dying. *What would you tell your child about the world if you only had five minutes left?* was the question he'd asked himself.

The result was the most mature, thoughtful song he'd ever written. Sometimes he couldn't quite believe he'd written it! But it was unmistakably his voice, his words, his thoughts and ideas. Knowing that this was the sort of thing he could create when let loose filled him with excitement.

For a long time, the album was going to be called *Pink*. Harry had read an interview with Paul Simonon, of the iconic punk band The Clash. He'd said that pink was the "only true rock n' roll colour" because it was the one that all the serious male rock musicians were scared to wear in case they looked "girly". Harry loved that. He'd always felt frustrated by the way some clothing was considered off-limits to men, and flaunting his lack of interest in strict gender boundaries was something he was keen to explore.

There was concern that people would mistake the album for one by P!nk, the popular singer from the early 2000s.

"Can't we just call the album *Sign of the Times* then?" asked Harry, as he was increasingly certain it would be the album's centrepiece track.

"I don't know," replied Bhasker. "I mean, it has been used." He's referring to *Sign O' The Times*, a 1987 album by Prince, and one of the most critically acclaimed records of all time.

"Oh yeah," Harry laughed. It was one of his favourite albums.

The two months in Jamaica seemed to both fly past and also last forever. Harry didn't want it to ever end, but he was also keen to share the songs with people. The album was taking shape, with ten tracks that he absolutely loved. Many of them had been inspired by his relationship with Kendall. Not always in terms of the lyrics being about her, but her influence, her outlook on things, kept inspiring Harry during the writing process.

Harry headed back home to England with a rough copy of the album. He'd listen to it over and over, making sure each song stood out and flowed naturally into the next. He knew he had the right songs, but it was just as important that they were in the right order. He hoped people would listen to it all the way through, not just shuffle through it.

Christmas in Holmes Chapel was a lot colder than the sunny beaches of Jamaica. Harry nervously balanced a cheap pair of speakers on a stool in his mum's living room and hit play. By the end, tears were streaming down her face. They were tears of relief.

"My biggest fear was that everything had happened so fast," she told him. "And what if the ride stopped suddenly after that? How could we support you through that?" These songs, so beautiful and personal and moving, had shown her that it didn't matter. *Even if nobody buys this album, this is the music I want to make*, Harry thought to himself, clasping her hand.

"I could spend the rest of my life doing this and I'd be the happiest man on the planet," he said. His mum smiledand replied: "That's all we ever wanted."

CHAPTER 18

READY, SET, RELEASE

Harry tapped 'send' and sat back, feeling a curious mix of satisfaction and excitement. He'd just posted the release date for 'Sign of the Times', his first single, to his millions of followers. It was a simple post – the name of the song and the date, 7 April 2017 – but it was the first official confirmation that his solo career was about to begin.

He flipped through to his phone's music app and tapped 'play'. He'd listened to the album, now simply called *Harry Styles*, dozens of times over. Now it was all done; the final production polish had been added, the running order agreed.

The first gentle guitar strums of 'Meet Me in the Hallway' played through Harry's earbuds. Opening the album with a quiet, acoustic song was a big gamble. This wasn't the sort of music people knew him for. But that was exactly why he'd chosen to start the album with it. It told the listener that One Direction pop was not on the menu!

Then came the piano-led 'Sign of the Times'. This song still sent a shiver down Harry's spine and made his heart soar when it reached its crescendo. He imagined playing this live, and how the crowd would react. He couldn't wait.

The funky groove of 'Carolina' led into the country twang of break-up song 'Two Ghosts'. The delicately plucked notes of 'Sweet Creature' came next, a folksy love song. These were two of the songs that Harry expected would send people crazy with theories about who he'd written them for. He wasn't going to tell, but this was one of the things he loved about the album – every single song, every single line, meant something to him. They were about real emotions he'd experienced.

A change of tempo next. The stomping boogie of 'Only Angel' followed by the hard rock riffs of 'Kiwi'. These were the dance-floor fillers. 'Kiwi', in particular, brought back fond memories. It was a track that had taken shape almost as a joke in the studio in Jamaica, a swaggering beast of a song that took every rock cliché and turned it up to maximum. The more they'd played it, the more he and the band had fallen in love with it. Mitch delivered a killer guitar solo for it, and suddenly it became a song that had to be on the album.

'Ever Since New York' added some 90s indie shuffle to the album, and was another song Harry knew would have people speculating about his relationship with Taylor. He didn't care. It was a lovely song, whoever people wanted to think it was about. The spoken intro to 'Woman' still made him giggle, and reminded him of the all night romcom marathons in the studio. The slow, stomping drumbeat thrilled him every time. And then, to close the album, 'From the Dining Room', another acoustic break-up ballad with an almost nursery rhyme rhythm to bring it full circle.

It was a great album. He felt it in his bones. For the first time in years, he couldn't wait to get out on tour. The prospect of spending months on the road, performing with the band, singing songs that came from his heart, made him smile from ear to ear.

'Sign of the Times' dropped on 7 April. Zayn, Niall and Louis had all debuted solo material before Harry, but that no longer mattered. It wasn't a race, and Harry had loved seeing his bandmates spreading their wings in their own ways. Zayn had even collaborated with Taylor Swift, which felt... weird. But Harry was philosophical about it all. People would either like his new songs or they wouldn't, but nobody could deny they were his songs.

'Sign of the Times' went straight to the top of the charts in the UK, which meant the world to Harry. It even knocked his old pal Ed Sheeran's 'Shape of You' off the top spot after an incredible 13 weeks. Then he was off on a whirlwind promotional tour. He appeared on *The Graham Norton* show, the first time he'd played solo on British TV, and then flew to the US to be the special guest on *Saturday Night Live*. He got to play Rolling Stones singer Mick Jagger (one of his heroes) in a sketch, which thrilled him.

The album was set to release on 12 May, and Harry built up to it with an appearance on *The Today*

Show, where One Direction had made their US debut. He got to play three album tracks – 'Carolina', 'Sign of the Times', and 'Ever Since New York' – and then threw in a solo performance of 'Stockholm Syndrome', one of the 1D songs he'd co-written. There'd been some debate with his manager and publicist about reminding people of his boy-band past so soon, but Harry wasn't bothered. Some of his former bandmates were going out of their way to distance themselves from their pop past. Harry was proud of it and wanted to reassure the fans that he shared their love for those years.

He was back in London for a small, intimate charity gig one day, then over in Los Angeles for another charity show at the iconic Troubadour venue days later. For that one he got to perform with rock legend Stevie Nicks of Fleetwood Mac, just one of the many dream-come-true moments he'd experience along the way.

Harry had become good friends with James Corden during the One Direction years, meeting him at lots of events and award ceremonies. James had taken over the US talk show *The Late Late*

Show in 2015, and Harry had become so close to the production team that he'd even lived with the show's producer and his wife in London for months while sorting out his own place. That friendship paid off as he got to do something no other act had ever done: he co-hosted the popular daily show alongside James not just for one night, but for a whole week. The PR blitz was exhausting, and it felt like the jetlag would never end, but it worked: *Harry Styles* went to number one in the UK and US.

The tour for the album was set to begin in September, but in June Harry received a call he'd been dreading. His stepdad, Robin, had died after a long battle with cancer. He'd been with Harry's mum, Anne, for years. Harry had even been the best man at their wedding in 2013, just as One Direction was at its peak. The 1D lads had all loved Robin, and he'd been one of their biggest supporters on social media. As the sad news spread, they all shared their condolences. Louis's message was particularly poignant. He'd lost his mum only months earlier. As thrilling as it was to be striking out on his own, Harry was moved by how quickly his bandmates rallied around him. He paused all his album promotion and went home to mourn with his mum and siblings. It was a cruel reminder that even when everything is going right, life can still hurt. Harry was more determined than ever to tackle fame on his own terms, to make the music he wanted to make and to make Robin proud.

CHAPTER 19

MADISON SQUARE GARDEN

The plan had always been for Harry's first solo tour – simply titled 'Live on Tour' – to be a smaller, more intimate experience but it quickly became clear that the fans had other ideas. It kicked off in San Francisco's Masonic Auditorium in September 2017, a venue for 3,000 people. By the time the tour came to an end in the summer of 2018, Harry was playing in arenas to fit everybody in. Even then, the shows were selling out – including New York's famous Madison Square Garden, which was attended by over 33,000 people!

More importantly for Harry, the tour raised a lot of money for charity. He'd been looking for ways to use his popularity to drive awareness of causes he believed in. In every country, he selected local charities who would benefit from each concert. In the USA, he used his concerts to encourage fans to register to vote, and made sure that the thousands of plastic water bottles left by fans were recycled.

Among the merch available for sale at every show were two T-shirts celebrating Pride, with the money raised helping to fund safe schools for LGBTQ children who were struggling. They bore the slogan 'Treat People with Kindness', a motto that summed up Harry's approach to life.

Along the way, Harry was thinking about his next album. The second album is a famously tricky one for artists. Stick too close to what people liked first time around and there was a risk fans would think that was all you had to offer. Change things too much and those fans might not come back at all. Harry decided to ignore all the music business superstitions and just follow his gut.

Having established his credibility as a songwriter on the first album, with its numerous ballads, he knew he wanted the next album to be a more upbeat offering. Something people could dance to, all the way through, but keeping just enough of that acoustic authenticity to avoid being empty pop for the club crowd.

Touring with the same band that he'd be recording with helped a lot. Between shows they'd toss ideas around and experiment with melodies as the songs took shape. The same production team also returned, led by Jeff Bhasker, but one new face on the scene was someone called Kid Harpoon.

He wasn't a kid! His real name was Tom Hull, and he was older than Harry by just over ten years. As well as writing and producing for other acts, including Florence + The Machine, Tom was a singer and songwriter himself. He and Harry hit if off straight away.

With the tour out of the way, Harry hurried back into the studio for the part of the pop star process he was starting to love more than any other. This time it was Malibu, California, where they retreated to work, with the laid-back party city perfectly matching the vibes Harry was looking for. After a long day, they'd lounge on the beach, listening to classic pop and rock albums. Of course, sometimes things would get a little too relaxed – like the night Harry managed to lose both his trousers and wallet in the sand! He got the wallet back after a kind member of the public found it but was heartbroken to never see his bright yellow corduroy trousers ever again!

Harry was determined to push his songwriting skills even further. Tom encouraged him to take up meditation and really explore his thoughts and feelings. When recording started in earnest, Harry was still hurting from the end of his year-long romance with a French model called Camille Rowe. It was Tom who told him to channel those feelings into his writing, advice that Harry took to heart. A voicemail from Camille was even woven into one of the songs, 'Cherry'.

While the album, which eventually got the name *Fine Line*, was shaping up to be a much more energetic collection of songs, Harry's lyrics were becoming more personal. On tracks such as 'Falling' and 'To Be So Lonely', Harry found himself exposing more of his deepest thoughts and fears than ever before. These weren't just break-up songs, they were songs in which Harry ruthlessly pulled apart his own failings and tormented himself over the mistakes he'd made in past relationships. It hurt, but it also felt good to be so raw and open.

Harry also relished being able to pursue his ideas, no matter how strange. One of the albums that was inspiring him was *Blue* by Joni Mitchell. The 1971 album featured a very distinctive string instrument called a dulcimer. Harry adored its sound so much that he didn't want to just buy a new dulcimer for the album. He tracked down the woman who had built the one used by Joni Mitchell and, after a long, exciting conversation, was able to buy and use the exact same instrument that had enchanted him. It was moments like that which made him pinch himself!

Just like his first album, Harry took his time getting *Fine Line* just right, working on it throughout 2018 and only starting to feel it was ready in the late summer of 2019. Between recording sessions, he threw himself into the celebrity lifestyle, thrilled by the opportunities that were coming his way.

In May 2019 he co-hosted the Met Gala with

Lady Gaga. One of the most famous and prestigious fashion events in the world, it was an occasion Harry had always loved for its flamboyance and flair, so being asked to be one of the hosts was a huge honour. Harry turned heads on the red carpet in a sheer black blouse designed by Gucci. He'd always loved dressing up, and found it hilarious — and a bit sad — that so many people felt weird about men wearing feminine clothing. It wasn't something he could have got away with as a member of One Direction, but now he was letting his tastes shine!

He even got to help produce a TV comedy inspired by his own experiences. *Happy Together* starred Australian actor Felix Mallard as a pop star who ends up living with his accountant in a normal suburban house. It was based on the time Harry spent living in the loft of Ben Winston, the British producer of James Corden's *The Late Late Show*, at the height of One Direction's fame. The story was changed a lot, but Harry still got to be involved in its development and learn even more about how another area of showbiz worked.

As the release date for *Fine Line* approached,

Harry had an idea for how he'd like to promote it. He still fondly remembered the viral video treasure hunt that had sent One Direction fans scouring the internet for clues to a missing laptop, and wondered if he could do something similar but with a particular upbeat message behind it.

That's why in early December, people were mystified by a big tourist marketing campaign for an island called Eroda, just off the coast of Scotland. Overnight there was a website, with a detailed history of the island and its many features and attractions. A hashtag – #VisitEroda – was all over social media. Printed brochures even turned up in New York. There was just one problem: Eroda didn't exist.

It was all Harry's idea, of course. Eroda – 'adore' spelled backwards – was a place he'd invented with his team of creatives, a place with a history that would tie in with his 'Be Kind to People' motto, as well as a map stuffed with hints about tracks on his upcoming album. His fans were ahead of the game, already swapping theories and digging out references and clues from across the internet, but all was revealed in the extended video for 'Adore You', the album's second single, released the week before the album. More of a short film than a music video, it featured Harry as a boy raised on the island, which was always shrouded in gloomy clouds. Shunned by the locals for his beaming smile, he instead befriends a rare stranded fish, singing the song's chorus as it outgrows the various makeshift homes Harry finds for it. In the end, with his beloved fish grown to giant size, all the Eroda villagers come together to help him return it to the sea, where it rejoins hundreds of other fish just like it.

The whole thing was funny and playful, full of silly moments, but the meaning behind it came straight from Harry's heart. We have to love each other, we have to look out for each other, if we're going to get through dark times.

Fine Line was released on 13 December and was yet another huge hit. Another world tour was planned to kick off in April 2020. But within just a few months the threat of a dangerous new virus, COVID-19, meant the world had to lock down. People couldn't leave their homes, let alone pack together in arenas for a concert. Everyone was suddenly isolated and scared. The message of Eroda was needed more than ever.

CHAPTER 20

FEATHER BOAS FOR EVERYONE

"I'm lucky because I'm staying in with friends, but we're checking on people all the time who are living on their own," Harry said. It was March 2020, a few weeks into lockdown, and he'd called in on FaceTime to Zane Lowe's Apple Music podcast. "It's a long time to be in your house," he added.

Harry kept a strict schedule in quarantine. This helped him maintain his mental and physical health, as well as keeping world events in perspective. He'd wake up early to meditate and read. Then he'd work out and go for a walk, before working on songs in the afternoon. In many ways this was the most freeform creative process he'd ever had. There was no album to work towards, no live performances. He was just practising piano and guitar, and writing poems, songs, anything that came into his head.

More singles were released from *Fine Line* to keep up the connection with his fans. He'd filmed a video for 'Watermelon Sugar' in January, before everything closed down, and the directors were worried that releasing a video showing people hanging out on a beach, hugging each other, would seem insensitive now that everyone was stuck indoors. Harry knew that it was exactly what people wanted to see. What they needed to see. A caption was added to the start – "this video is dedicated to touching". The song went on to become Harry's first solo number one in America.

The long, enforced break had rewired Harry's approach to his music. He was still learning to let go of the nagging voice that insisted he had to keep putting new stuff out, and he thought more and more about his favourite artists – the quirky rock stars of the 60s and 70s – who would sometimes disappear for years, then come back with something completely unexpected, and it was a huge event. He was drawn more and more to that idea.

For now, though, he'd spent long enough chipping away at the next album. It felt ready and it felt like it was time. He had a clear vision of what album number three would be. All those months of seclusion and introspection had convinced him that he wanted to invite people into his mind, into his house, and really share things at a level of intimacy that even his first two albums hadn't come close to. *Harry's House* was the perfect title for what he had in mind.

Some of the songs were ones that had been kicking around for a long time. 'Boyfriends' had started out as a track that could have appeared on *Fine Line*. He'd written an early version of 'Little Freak' in a Tokyo hotel room in 2019. Something had told him they weren't right yet, though. It was only now, with a more focused understanding of what he wanted to say as an artist, that he saw how and where they could fit on this new album.

Harry was also becoming more comfortable with taking inspiration from the most unlikely places. 'Matilda' was named after the Roald Dahl book and written for a female friend who was feeling as alone as the title character. 'Music for a Sushi Restaurant' came about after hearing one of his own songs playing in an actual sushi restaurant! He was confident enough in his creative instincts to grab these sparks and turn them into something meaningful in the studio. Reunited with Kid Harpoon and his regular band, Harry polished the songs until he was absolutely happy with them. This one would be special. He knew it.

His team kept a close eye on the laws surrounding lockdowns and when they would be lifted, but in the end he couldn't tour *Fine Line* until September 2021, almost two whole years after the album came out. Once the restrictions were lifted, he made up for lost time. His first album tour had been called 'Harry Styles: Live on Tour'. It only made sense, after everything, that this would be 'Love on Tour'. That was what he wanted everyone to feel. This had to be a celebration!

His 2021 New York dates at the enormous Madison Square Garden went ahead at the end of October, so with typical playful inspiration he decided they would be 'Harryween' fancy dress concerts and encouraged the tens of thousands of fans to come in costume. Harry, cheekily, dressed as Dorothy from *The Wizard of Oz*!

'Love on Tour' finished its first North American leg at the UBS Arena in Long Island, New York, on 28 November. Harry had played 42 shows in just two months! Even with his hectic schedule, he somehow also found time to launch his own range of beauty products called *Pleasing*. At his insistence, they were marketed as gender neutral and designed to complement people's natural beauty, not smother it in heavy make-up.

Harry was ready for some personal time, although that still involved a lot of travel. He had been dating actor-director Olivia Wilde since early 2021 after they'd met during filming for one of Olivia's films. Now they planned to spend Christmas together, while visiting both their families – Olivia's parents in Virginia and Harry's mum Anne in London – over the holiday break.

Refreshed and ready for action, Harry threw himself into 2022, which was already shaping up to be a life-changing year. The first few months were spent finishing off *Harry's House*, which was due to release in May. Just before then he'd been asked to headline the Coachella festival in April, the biggest gig of his life. Even though it was technically still the same tour launched to promote *Fine Line*, he loved being able to introduce a whole new album's worth of songs to his set and see fans reactions to his latest music live.

Anticipation for the album was at fever pitch when *Harry's House* went on sale on 22 May. It was a monster hit, going straight to number one not just in the USA and UK, but in 12 other countries as well – including Australia, Canada, even Switzerland! Both the album and the singles released from it were so popular that at one point Harry had four songs in America's Billboard Top 10 at the same time! He was the first British solo artist in history to achieve this amazing feat.

'Love on Tour' resumed in the summer, taking him all over the UK, across Europe, and then to the USA. As summer turned to autumn, he was back at Madison Square Garden for a record-breaking 15-show residency that would take up most of August and September.

At the end of his fifteenth Madison Square Garden concert in a row, Harry was presented with a special banner from the owners of the iconic concert venue. The banner was then raised into the rafters of the hall, where it still hangs to this day. Only two other music acts have ever been honoured in this way – singer-songwriter Billy Joel and the rock band Phish. Harry accepted the honour in his own unique style: everyone in the audience was given a free feather boa to wear!

Later in 2022 people would see more of Harry as an actor, but even starring alongside girlfriend Olivia Wilde couldn't save their relationship and they broke up at the end of 2022. Harry wasn't sure if he'd do any more acting. As much as he enjoyed the creative challenge while the cameras were rolling, there was a lot of waiting around on set, feeling bored and useless. At times like that, he wished he was back in the studio with a guitar and a notebook, where he could put the downtime to better use and keep making stuff.

It was a head-spinning period of activity, but a

rewarding one. Having the tour to keep coming back to helped keep it all focused. That was where he felt alive. On stage, feeling the love from fans and reflecting it back to them, bonded through music.

In February 2023, Harry ticked off another important milestone. In front of an audience made up of the biggest names in the music industry, *Harry's House* was named Album of the Year at the Grammy Awards. Harry's album had been chosen over the latest releases from huge stars like Beyonce, Coldplay and Adele. Making the moment even more special, his name was read out on stage by Reina Lafantaisie, a grandma from Ontario, Canada, who had been invited to the ceremony because she was such a big Harry fan! Harry, still a little stunned by the win, raced up the steps onto the stage and gave her a massive hug before giving a humble starstruck speech.

"There's no such thing as 'best' in music," he insisted, praising the other acts nominated alongside him. There couldn't be a more Harry way of winning!

With that stunning victory to drive him onwards, 'Love on Tour' made its way down through South

America, before jetting back to Europe for the final run of shows. The last concert took place in July 2023, at Italy's massive RCF Arena, the biggest concert venue in Europe. 100,000 fans came out to see him, and as he left the stage to thunderous applause and cheers, he realised there was finally nothing lined up to follow. No studios booked. No gigs to play. Just time to himself, to experiment, to really sit down and concentrate on his music for no other reason than the love of doing it.

He thought back to those singers he idolised, whose songs he'd sung with his mum on the drive to school, who he'd danced to on the radio while working in the bakery back in Holmes Chapel. Many of those rock legends were now his friends, something that continued to blow his mind.

He thought about how they'd vanish from the spotlight and only return when they had something new to share. They were confident and comfortable enough in their talent to just take their time. That sounded like a pretty great idea right now. Sure, the press would still follow him around, photos of him in cafes with girlfriends would still circulate on social media, but in terms of what he was doing next, when he'd be ready with even more new songs, that would be a mystery – to himself as much as the fans. With the love from those fans still ringing in his ears, he smiled all the way back to his dressing room, ready to see where life would take him next...

Turn the page for a sneak preview of another

inspiring Ultimate Superstars story...

SABRINA CARPENTER

AVAILABLE NOW!

CHAPTER 1

SWIFTIE TO BESTIE

Sabrina had just received one of the most important calls of her career.

"Taylor wants me to open for her!" Her eyes were wide with disbelief. When she was a little girl she put posters of Miley Cyrus, Ariana Grande, Selena Gomez and Taylor Swift on her bedroom walls. Now Taylor wanted Sabrina to join her on the 'Eras Tour. "Just wait until I tell the fans!" But for now, it was top secret.

Sabrina was so excited. It felt like yesterday that she was sat in her bedroom with only her guitar, painstakingly learning the chords to Taylor's 'Picture to Burn'. One time her dad peeked in and asked her what she was doing.

"I'm practising for when I'm famous," she said with a grin. She was only ten, but she knew what she wanted even then.

Fourteen years later, that dream was a reality – although it did feel unreal. Sabrina was no longer a girl with posters; she was living alongside her idols, one of whom had become a friend and another who she had performed alongside: Ariana. By May 2023, rumours about Sabrina and Taylor's friendship were swirling, fuelled by photos and social media interactions. Then came Sabrina's trip to Philadelphia for Taylor's concert.

What a night that was. The show was everything Sabrina had imagined and more. Sitting with her sister Sarah in the packed stadium, she found herself singing along to every word and laughing when Taylor joked about her cats. The choreography and emotional storytelling made her jaw drop.

"She makes it look effortless," Sabrina whispered.

Sarah nudged her. "You're next, you know."

Sabrina rolled her eyes. "Yeah, right."

"Just wait," Sarah replied, with a knowing smile.

On 2 June 2023, Sabrina posted an announcement on Instagram that sent her fans into a frenzy. It read:

trying to process this but alas i shant CANT WAIT TO JOIN THE ERAS TOUR IN LATIN AMERICA thank u @taylorswift u the 1 :') this is a dream come true

Within hours, the internet was exploding with excitement. Fans reposted the announcement and the comments section lit up with messages like:

This is your spot... Shine girl!

Sabrina had every intention of shining. She went straight into rehearsals; there was no time to chill after the spill!

"This is huge," Sabrina FaceTimed Sarah. "I've got to get it right."

"You will," Sarah assured her. She always had Sabrina's back.

"This is my big break. I have got this!"

The first show where Sabrina opened for Taylor

was in Mexico City on 24 August 2023. Standing backstage, she had that familiar feeling – sick to the pit of her stomach with nerves! The arena was packed with Swifties, *but hopefully there are a few Carpenters out there too*, Sabrina thought to herself and crossed her fingers behind her back. She adjusted her microphone pack and glanced in the mirror. She felt sassy in her platform boots and black sequin outfit.

"You have got this, Sabrina Carpenter," she repeated to herself, flicking her hair back with all the self-assurance of a seasoned star!

As the lights dimmed, Sabrina heard her name being announced. The crowd erupted – Sabrina had a big following in Mexico City. She beamed, she needed to hear the cheers. It drove her on. She stepped onto the stage, launching into 'Feather', the song which had hit number one on the US *Billboard* Pop Songs chart earlier that year. When Sabrina saw the audience joining in and dancing, she knew she had them – that's when she went into overdrive.

"Don't forget Selena," Sabrina told the crowd as she began singing 'Dreaming of You' by American Tejano singer Selena Quintanilla-Pérez. The Tex-Mex singer had passed away in 1995, and the Mexican crowd appreciated Sabrina's nod to the star. There were tears and huge cheers as Sabrina hit the final note. She looked across the auditorium and felt the love, the connection and the magic.

By the time Sabrina got to 'Nonsense', the audience was completely in sync with her energy, laughing at her funny ad-libs and singing along to the chorus.

"I love you guys," she told them warmly, her eyes sparkling with mischievous excitement, as she said her farewells after singing an encore.

"Wow, that was the performance of my life!" Sabrina told Taylor later that night.

"Oh girl," Taylor said, giving Sabrina a gentle nudge. "The best is yet to come for you!"

The *Eras Tour* took Sabrina to thirteen shows in Latin America, followed by six in Australia and another six in Singapore. Each night was a new adventure and Sabrina adapted her performances to the unique energy of each audience. In Brazil, she was overwhelmed by the party atmosphere kicked up by the fans, who sang every word of her songs with passion.

"It's like they're performing for me," she joked backstage.

Tour life wasn't without its challenges. Sabrina's hit 'Nonsense', known for its cheeky and sometimes risqué lyrics, required a little tweaking for family-friendly crowds.

"I had to tone it down a little tonight," she admitted to the crew in Singapore. "But I still kept it fun!"

Sitting in her hotel room after a show, Sabrina scrolled through fan videos of her performances. One caption really caught her eye:

Sabrina Carpenter: The Taylor Swift of her generation.

Sabrina smiled, her eyes misting over with emotion. It was a bold comparison, a HUGE compliment, and it spoke to how far she'd come. She felt proud.

"The best is yet to come, huh?" Sabrina thought, curling up in the super king size bed. Every muscle in her body ached after the performance. And man her feet were on fire after dancing in those boots! But, she didn't care, she was doing the thing she loved best in the world. It felt like she was on course to something bigger than she ever dreamed possible. Her head was swirling with happy thoughts as she fell into a deep, deep sleep – with a cheeky grin on her face.